a year in the garden

a year in the garden

a step-by-step guide to vital gardening projects through the year

Steven Bradley

photography by
Anne Hyde

RYLAND
PETERS
& SMALL
LONDON NEW YORK

For this edition:

Senior Designer Amy Trombat

Senior Editor Clare Double

Picture Research Emily Westlake

Production Sheila Smith, Simon Walsh

Publishing Director Alison Starling

US Consultant David Grist

Illustrators David Ashby, Leslie Craig, Sarah Kensington, Amanda Patton,
Polly Raynes, Gill Tomblin, Ann Winterbotham

First published in the United States in 2001.

This new edition published in 2007 by Ryland Peters & Small

519 Broadway, 5th Floor

New York, NY 10012

www.rylandpeters.com

10 9 8 7 6 5 4 3 2 1

Material contained in this book was originally published
in *Getting Ready for Winter* (published in 1997), *Waking Up the
Garden*, and *Keeping the Garden in Bloom* (both published in 1998).

Library of Congress Cataloging-in-Publication Data

Bradley, Steve, 1949-

A year in the garden : a step-by-step guide to vital gardening projects through
the year / Steven Bradley ; photography by Anne Hyde. -- First U.S. ed.

p. cm.

Includes index.

ISBN-13: 978-1-84597-357-5

ISBN-10: 1-84597-357-7

1. Gardening. I. Hyde, Anne. II. Title.

SB450.97.B73 2007

635--dc22

2006031339

contents

The gardening year begins in early spring and carries through until the first hard frosts of late fall herald a period of dormancy for most plants. It is not possible to be precise about when specific tasks need to be undertaken, since so much depends not only on the prevailing climatic conditions where you live, but also on the microclimate that prevails in your garden. It is possible, however, to divide the gardening year into three principal seasons of activity.

Spring can be a stressful period. Too much to do, too little time to do it—and, of course, the plants can't wait to get started. Your timing is critical—how do you get the earliest possible start while beating those lingering spring frosts? Day temperatures can soar for hours at a time before plunging to freezing overnight. Strong winds thrash young foliage and heavy rain batters tender seedlings; nevertheless, we are glad when spring finally arrives.

Spring provides a perfect opportunity to create something new —a short-term project, perhaps, such as planting a hanging basket for a summer display, or something more permanent, such as planting a climber to provide years of interest. Spring is also the time to renovate any shrubs that need pruning to stimulate new growth. The lawn, too, can look sad after the ravages of winter. Now is the time to undertake repairs, deal with any moss, and begin feeding, weeding, and mowing to encourage grass growth. Start the season by carrying out any repairs on machinery and equipment before they are needed for the coming year.

Summer is often the most colorful time of year in the garden. Growth is still rapid, and in order to sustain it, much of this season's work is aimed at keeping plants watered and fed. At times, it may feel as if the gardener has to run in order to stand still. The lawn grows overnight and needs constant mowing; hedges need clipping

at every turn; blooms need deadheading, young fruit trees need training, and no sooner has one batch of seeds been sown than another batch of seedlings needs thinning or staking. Regardless of all the hard labor, summer is also a time when the garden can be enjoyed at close quarters. The warm weather and lingering daylight hours entice us outdoors for long periods; but even when they are apparently simply relaxing, experienced gardeners are using their time to note successful plants and planting schemes, and to record any failures or disappointments for moving or disposal. This helps to make sure that the same mistakes are not made next year, when the glorious technicolor experiment can be tried all over again.

Fall signals a change of direction—as exciting as the other seasons, but in different ways. As the growing season draws to a close, the process of shutting down the garden for the winter begins, with annuals dying back and perennials storing food for the winter months to come. The shorter days also bring about some pretty dramatic changes, with many deciduous plants, and a few evergreen ones, really making their presence felt in a glorious display of color.

Fall is a time for looking back on the year and noting successes and failures. Plans can be made now while the events are still fresh in the mind, because much of the work done in fall will determine the success of the coming year. Cleaning the garden is a good way to begin. Prune unwanted branches and twigs, and shred them into bags as a mulch for next year. Clear away all annuals that have died down, and dig beds and plots to bury weeds and plant debris. This helps to eliminate pest and disease problems, and provides vital organic matter. Rather than being the end of the present growing season, fall should be regarded as the beginning of the new one.

Steven Bradley

new introductions

The prospect of adding new plants to the garden is irresistible. Either the acquisition of new plants or raising them from seed or cuttings for that little space in the garden will always be a source of excitement. There is a great sense of anticipation, too, as ideas for new planting schemes take shape, perhaps inspired by the vast range of plants on show at garden centers or in other people's backyards. The challenge may be to produce a display that changes with the seasons, providing interest and color all year round. What often determines when new plants are introduced is their hardiness and growth patterns. In truth, there can be overlap in the gardening tasks that are carried out in the different seasons, especially between fall and spring.

planting bulbs

"Bulb" is a generic term that is often loosely used to describe bulbous plants such as bulbs, corms, rhizomes, and tubers. Although most bulbs found in the average garden will have been propagated in Europe, they may have originated from as far afield as South Africa, South America, the Mediterranean, or even the Middle East. The planting and maintenance of bulbs is relatively straightforward, but care when planting is important to guarantee complete success. Most soil types are suitable, but try to avoid soil that remains waterlogged during winter. Consider location when you choose your bulbs; most prefer a sunny position, but some, such as snowdrops (*Galanthus*), prefer to grow in the dappled shade given by trees.

tools and equipment

Trowel
This is the most popular planting tool for small plants and is probably the best one to use if only a few bulbs are to be planted, or if the bulbs being planted vary greatly in size.

Spade
A garden spade is the best tool to use for planting a large number of bulbs, or planting bulbs in groups.

Bulb planter
A hand-held bulb planter (almost a trowel with a circular blade) is useful where several bulbs are to be planted at the same time. This tool removes a core of soil, leaving a hole into which the bulb is placed. A larger version with a spadelike shaft and handle is useful where the soil is hard or heavy with clay. The main disadvantage of bulb planters is that all of the holes are the same size.

how deep to plant

Depth is particularly important when planning a display of bulbs, because inconsistent planting will lead to uneven flowering, which can spoil the effect of mass groupings of bulbs. Depending on the bulbs being planted, the depth can vary from as shallow as ½ inch to as deep as 10 inches. See below for correct depths.

By planting bulbs fractionally deeper than the recommended depth, however, flowering can be delayed by up to ten days. A useful technique is to plant half your bulbs at the correct depth and the other half of the bulbs slightly deeper; the flowering display of one particular cultivar can then be extended over a longer period.

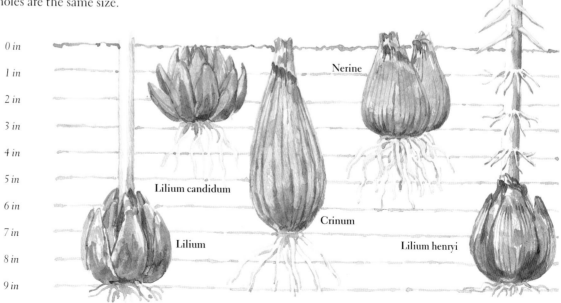

0 in
1 in
2 in
3 in
4 in
5 in
6 in
7 in
8 in
9 in

Nerine

Lilium candidum

Crinum

Lilium

Lilium henryi

planting a single bulb

Bulbs often look their best planted in groups, but some of the larger-flowering types, such as the giant onions (*Alliums*), make a fine display when planted individually. The bulb planter below is ideal to use when introducing bulbs between established plants.

1   Push the bulb planter or trowel into the ground with a twisting motion to cut through the soil, rather than forcing it straight in.

2   After making the planting hole, break up the soil in the bottom with a trowel.

3   Set the bulb in the hole in an upright position, then fill with soil until the surface is level. Pack the soil gently.

grouping

Make a shallow trench, then position the bulbs in the bottom. Refill the trench and pack the soil gently.

naturalizing bulbs

To achieve a random, natural look for a group of bulbs growing in grass, scatter a handful of bulbs over the grass and plant them where they land.

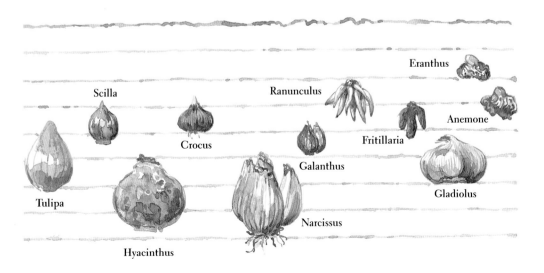

Eranthus

Scilla

Ranunculus

Anemone

Crocus

Fritillaria

Galanthus

Tulipa

Gladiolus

Narcissus

Hyacinthus

late-flowering bulbs

Bulbs that are intended to flower in the summer and fall must have a soil that retains plenty of moisture through the summer months while they are growing. However, the soil must also be free-draining during the winter to prevent the bulbs from rotting while they are dormant. Late-flowering bulbs are ideal for planting in mixed beds, where they can be used to extend the season of interest and give the bed an "early start." Bulbs can be selected to develop and flower before many of the shrubs and herbaceous perennials have started to show color. Another added attraction of some summer- and fall-flowering bulbs is that the seed heads can be kept after the blooms are finished. For example, ornamental onions (*Alliums*) are particularly valuable for this purpose. The old seed heads can either be left in situ, where they will last well into the winter, or they can be cut down, hung to dry, and used in dried-flower arrangements.

Gladiolus tristis 'Bowlby'

Alstroemeria

Lilium candidum

Lilium 'Enchantment'

Colchicum 'The Giant'

Amaryllis belladonna

Cyclamen hederifolium

Allium

preparing for planting

Bulbs that grow and flower later in the year frequently have to endure some of the driest growing conditions and will often root quite deeply into the soil to find moisture. Incorporating generous quantities of well-rotted organic matter before planting will aid moisture retention. Bulbs are normally sold and planted while they are dry, with no roots or leaves. However, snowdrops (*Galanthus*) will establish better if transplanted almost immediately after flowering, "in the green" (see right) with the leaves still present, when new roots are produced very quickly.

Summer- and fall-flowering bulbs

Calla lily (*Zantedeschia aethiopica*)

Crocosmia

Foxtail lily (*Eremurus*)

Giant lily (*Cardiocrinum*)

Gladiolus

Lily (*Lilium*)

Onion (*Allium*)

Peruvian lily (*Alstroemeria*)

Schizostylis coccinea

Sorrel (*Oxalis*)

planting in baskets

Any type of bulb can be planted in a wire or plastic basket. This is a clever device to use if you wish to move your plants; for instance in preparation for lifting, dividing, and storing once the foliage has died off, or for tender bulbs that need to be put indoors over winter.

1   Line the bottom of the basket with enough soil so that the bulbs will be planted at their correct depth. Then position the bulbs you have chosen on top of the layer of soil, spacing them out evenly.

2   Fill the basket with soil and lower it into a hole, deep enough so that the top rim sits just below soil level. Cover the top of the basket with soil and mark its position.

3   After planting, cover the area with a mulch of sharp gravel—this will deter slugs and snails from eating the shoots as they emerge, because they do not like traveling across sharp surfaces, and applying such a barrier also reduces the need to use chemical baits.

storing bulbs for replanting

1   Carefully lift "old" spring bulbs and leave in a cool, dry place for two or three days before brushing off any soil. Trim old roots and loose papery scales, and remove the dried stems level with the bulb neck.

2   Gently pull away any bulblets from around the mother bulb; these can be used to grow new plants. Discard soft or unusually light bulbs, because they may be infested with nematodes or bulb fly maggots, or be decaying due to damage caused by fungal rot.

3   Using clean, shallow trays or boxes lined with paper, arrange the bulbs in a single layer and put them in a cool, dry place until it is time for replanting in the fall. Inspect the bulbs every two or three weeks and immediately discard any that show signs of fungal rot or softness; otherwise, the surrounding bulbs may become infected.

planting annuals and biennials

These plants provide an enormous variety of flower color, form, and foliage texture, making them ideal candidates for planting in containers and hanging baskets; in the garden soil, they can be used to great effect massed in a bed by themselves, or as fillers between shrubs and other permanent plants. By choosing suitable species and cultivars, it is possible to have flowers for a large part of the year. Often, half-hardy annuals are used for summer color because they are very fast growing and provide an amazing display, which may last until the first frosts of fall or early winter.

planting for a summer display

Many summer bedding plants are half-hardy annuals whose seeds, if left to themselves, would not germinate until the early summer. Sowing seed in trays of potting medium in spring and keeping them in a greenhouse or on a warm windowsill means the plants will start growing early. Once the seedlings are large enough to touch without risk of damage, they can be transplanted from the seed trays into small pots. This will give them the space and food they need to keep growing quickly. Gradually harden them off (get them used to being outside) before planting them in their flowering site.

Transplanting (pricking out) seedlings

1   Select several small pots and fill to the top with pre-moistened potting soil. Firm the soil gently until it is ½ inch below the rim.

2   Using a label or similar utensil, gently tease the seedlings from the soil. Do this when the soil is slightly moist.

3   Make a hole with a dibble in the center of each pot. Then, lifting the seedlings individually, place each one, root first, into a hole.

4   Water gently to settle the soil around the roots. Label the pots with the plant name and date, then place in a shaded spot.

5   For plants destined to go into troughs and tubs, grow in 3-inch plastic pots and plunge them into the decorative container. The plant's roots will grow through the bottom of the pot into the potting medium.

6   After flowering, the plant can easily be removed by twisting the pot from side to side to sever any roots that have pushed through the drainage holes. You can then drop a replacement plant neatly into the hole.

planting for a spring display

As well as annuals, many hardy biennials are grown through the fall and winter. They are usually sown in a seedbed during early summer, transplanted into a nursery bed six or eight weeks later, and planted in display beds in the middle of the fall.

Sowing seed outdoors

The seeds are sown in straight lines, or drills, so the seedlings are in rows about 8 inches apart. A groove is cut in the soil (the depth depends on the seed involved) and the seed scattered along the bottom of the drill. Seeds should be sown as thinly as possible to reduce the need for thinning seedlings later. Sowing in drills is most commonly used for plants grown in nursery beds and transplanted later into permanent positions.

Lifting and transplanting

1   Lift the seedlings with a hand fork to avoid injuring the roots and hold them by their leaves. Draw plants raised in pots gently from the container. (Seedlings in biodegradable pots can be planted in the bed—pot and all.)

2   Start by digging a planting hole large enough to accommodate the root system. Hold the plant by its leaves, and place it in the hole with the roots spread out evenly.

3   Using a trowel, pull the soil back into the hole around the plant and firm gently. Clear the soil around the base of the plant so there is a slight depression around the stem.

4   Check that the plant is firm by gently pulling a leaf in an upward direction. The leaf may snap, but the plant should stay firmly in the soil. Finally, water around the base of the plant, filling up the depression.

seasonal interest

The spring season provides you with a perfect opportunity to create a short-term bedding display that will provide splashes of color in spaces that will eventually be filled by more permanent plantings. Interest in the garden can also be provided by sowing patches of annual grasses between other established plants. The gentle swaying and rustling of seed heads add an extra dimension. The easiest way to grow annuals and biennials is to sow them directly into the ground outside. This is done at the beginning of spring when the soil is starting to warm up again. For detailed instructions on planting annual seeds outdoors, see page 80.

Annuals and biennials for spring sowing	Season of interest	Height
Baby's breath (*Gypsophila paniculata*)	summer	4 feet
Bachelor's buttons (*Centaurea*)	summer	3 feet
Black-eyed Susan (*Rudbeckia hirta*)	summer	1–3 feet
Candytuft (*Iberis*)	late spring/summer	8–12 inches
Canterbury bells (*Campanula medium*)	spring/summer	2–3 feet
China aster (*Callistephus*)	summer	15–24 inches
Chinese forget-me-not (*Cynoglossum*)	spring/summer	12–18 inches
English daisy (*Bellis*)	spring/summer	4–6 inches
Flax (*Linum*)	summer	15 inches
Flowering tobacco (*Nicotiana*)	summer/fall	12–24 inches
Foxglove (*Digitalis*)	summer	3–5 feet
Godetia grandiflora	summer	12–16 inches
Hollyhock (*Alcea ficifolia*)	summer	8 feet
Love-in-a-mist (*Nigella*)	summer	18–30 inches
Mallow (*Lavatera trimestris*)	summer	4 feet
Money plant (*Lunaria annua*)	spring/summer	30 inches
Morning glory (*Ipomoea purpurea*)	summer/late fall	10 feet
Nasturtium (*Tropaeolum majus*)	summer	12–15 inches
Pansy (*Viola*)	spring/fall	6–8 inches
Poppy (*Papaver*)	summer	8–18 inches
Pot marigold (*Calendula officinalis*)	summer	12–28 inches
Siberian wallflower (*Erysimum allionii*)	late spring/summer	12 inches
Snapdragon (*Antirrhinum*)	summer	8–24 inches
Stock (*Matthiola incana*)	summer	32 inches
Sunflower (*Helianthus*)	late summer/fall	2–10 feet
Sweet William (*Dianthus barbatus*)	summer	28 inches
Treasure flower (*Gazania hybrida*)	summer/late fall	8–12 inches

Annual and biennial grasses for spring sowing	Season of interest	Height
Corn (*Zea mays*)	summer	3–4 feet
Fountain grass (*Pennisetum setaceum*)	summer	3 feet
Hare's tail (*Lagurus ovatus*)	summer	18 inches
Job's tears (*Coix lacryma-jobi*)	autumn	18–36 inches
Quaking grass (*Briza maxima*)	summer	20 inches
Squirrel tail grass (*Hordeum jubatum*)	summer	1 foot
Switch grass (*Panicum virgatum*)	fall	3 feet

Dianthus barbatus

Lavatera trimestris

Lunaria annua

planting for springtime color

After what often seems like a long, bleak, and colorless winter, there are few more heartening sights than flowers beginning to emerge from the soil to create bright patches of color amid the otherwise drab surroundings and bare-limbed trees. So, spring bedding plants are one of the most rewarding, as well as one of the easiest and most problem-free, groups of plants for the gardener to grow. An ideal mix includes bulbs, biennials, and low-growing perennials, selected for their display qualities.

Crocus

Muscari and *Narcissus*

planting out in spring

Seed to sow indoors	Scarlet sage (*Salvia splendens*)	Daffodil (*Narcissus*)
Aubrieta	Siberian wallflower (*Erysimum allionii*)	Grape hyacinth (*Muscari*)
Begonia	Wallflower (*Erysimum cheiri*)	*Iris reticulata*
English daisy (*Bellis*)		Marigold (*Calendula*)
Forget-me-not (*Myosotis*)	**Seed to sow outdoors**	Ornamental cabbage (*Brassica oleracea*)
Pansy (*Viola*)	Candytuft (*Iberis*)	Poppy (*Papaver*)
Primrose (*Primula*)	*Clarkia*	
Rock cress (*Arabis*)	*Crocus*	

Hardening off

Plants suitable for spring bedding that have been raised from seeds sown indoors, and young plants that have not reached maturity, have soft and sappy tissues that may easily be damaged if they are too suddenly exposed to low temperatures or cold, dry winds. To prevent this from happening, these plants must first be hardened off, or acclimatized, for up to two weeks before they can be successfully transplanted outdoors. Move them from the greenhouse or kitchen windowsill into a cold frame, or place them under cloches. Cloches covered in lightweight plastic must have their edges buried in the soil to prevent the cover from blowing off. Then, increase the amount of ventilation plants receive a little each day. Feed the plants with a suitable fertilizer—one that is low in nitrogen and high in potassium—to promote harder growth and protect them from the cold.

Plants grown outdoors

Some spring bedding plants can be raised and grown in seedbeds in the open ground rather than as bedding plants in a greenhouse or cold frame. They can be treated as usual as annuals and hardy biennials (see page 18). Seeds are sown in early summer, replanted in nursery beds, and then transferred to their permanent flowering sites in early fall. Water the plants several hours before they are to be moved.

perennials

These can be planted in spring or fall. Planting them in the fall means they can be put in soil that is still warm from the summer, which gives them a head start in spring when the weather improves. However, in very cold climates and for tender perennials, it is more sensible to leave planting until spring. Tender perennials include pincushion flower (*Scabiosa*), cardinal flower (*Lobelia cardinalis*), and pinks. Bear in mind that what is an annual or biennial in one climate could be a perennial in another, so there may be some overlap between plant categories.

plant selection

Before you begin planting, plan the site, taking into account the size of the plot and the relationship of the various plants. Also consider the timing as well as the suitability of your soil. Look for plants with strong, healthy growth buds at the base of the plant.

Spring planting	Season of interest	Height
Aster amellus	summer	20 inches
Blanket flower (*Gaillardia*)	summer	18–24 inches
Blazing star (*Liatris*)	summer	4 feet
Brunnera	spring	18 inches
Bugloss (*Anchusa*)	summer	20 inches
Campion (*Lychnis*)	summer	6–12 inches
Catnip (*Nepeta*)	summer	16–32 inches
Comfrey (*Symphytum*)	spring	10–20 inches
Delphinium	summer	3–6 feet
Hedge nettle (*Stachys*)	spring/summer	6–18 inches
Ligularia	summer	4 feet
Lungwort (*Pulmonaria*)	spring	10 inches
Oleander (*Nerine*)	fall	24 inches
Pearly everlasting (*Anaphalis*)	late summer	24 inches
Phlox	summer	4–12 inches
Pincushion flower (*Scabiosa*)	spring/summer	1–3 feet
Poppy (*Papaver*)	summer	8–18 inches
Red-hot poker (*Kniphofia*)	summer	3–6 feet
Spurge (*Euphorbia*)	summer	6½–13 feet
Sedum	summer	2–8 inches
Tanacetum syn. *Pyrethrum*	summer	12–30 inches
Fall planting	**Season of interest**	**Height**
African blue lily (*Agapanthus*)	mid- to late summer	39 inches
Baby's breath (*Gypsophila paniculata*)	midsummer	3 feet
Bear's breeches (*Acanthus spinosus*)	mid- to late summer	39 inches
Bleeding heart (*Dicentra spectabilis*)	late spring	24 inches
Elephant's ears (*Bergenia*)	early to mid-spring	12 inches
Giant kale (*Crambe cordifolia*)	summer	6½ feet
Lenten rose (*Helleborus orientalis*)	spring	18 inches
New England aster (*Aster novi-belgii*)	late summer	18–30 inches
Peony (*Paeonia lactiflora*)	early to midsummer	24–36 inches
Plantain lily (*Hosta*)	midsummer	12–30 inches
Regal lily (*Lilium regale*)	midsummer	3 feet
Sedum spectabile	early fall	24 inches
Winter iris (*Iris unguicularis*)	winter	12 inches

preparing the soil and planting perennials

Herbaceous perennials usually occupy the same site for three years, so soil must be well cultivated before planting. Test the pH and adjust it, if necessary, to a level of 6.5–7.0. Increase acidity (lower pH) by adding ground sulphur, or raise alkalinity by adding lime.

Planting depths

1   Plants with a fibrous root system should have the topmost root about ½ inch below soil level.

2   Those with a thick fleshy root, or a cluster or crown of buds, should be around 1 inch below soil level.

3   In soils that are prone to waterlogging, the base should be planted slightly above the soil level to avoid rotting.

Container-grown plants

1   Before planting, water the container thoroughly to moisten the plant's roots. Then dig a hole for the plant large enough to accommodate the roots.

2   Take the plant by its stem or leaves, gently lift it from the container, and remove the top ½ inch of soil from the surface and discard it (to get rid of weed seeds and moss).

3   Hold the plant by its root ball and carefully place it in the bottom of the hole.

4   With a trowel, pull the soil back into the hole around the plant and firm in place. Cover the soil, leaving a small depression around the stem.

5   Finally, water around the base, making sure you fill the depression.

Bare-root plants

The method for planting bare-root perennials is similar to that of transplanting seedlings. Follow the steps here, and for illustrated reference see steps 2, 3, and 4 on page 18.

1 Dig a hole large enough for the plant's root system; place the plant in the hole.

2 Pull the soil back into the hole around the plant and pack it down gently.

3 Leave a slight depression around the stem and check that the plant is secure.

4 Water around the base of the plant, filling the depression made earlier.

creating an instant display

It is generally best to plant perennials in fall or winter, but to see them in flower and close to their ultimate height and spread, you can buy and plant them in the summer. This is invaluable if you need to fill a gap in a group of plants, or want to hide another, perhaps early-flowering perennial that is no longer looking its best. It is useful, too, if you are planning a new bed from scratch, as you can get a clear impression of how the plants will look together. There is no need to stick to the rule of putting the shortest plants at the front of the bed, and the tallest ones at the back—a change in height often lends extra interest. When planting in summer, water carefully until the plants are established.

color schemes

There are numerous ways of using color to create a theme within a garden display. You can, for instance, give a bed a rainbow theme, starting at one end with plants that have flower colors in shades of violet, merging into blue, and changing through green and yellow to orange and red. This may be effective for a long bed, giving it a feeling of harmony and drawing the eye easily from end to end. Another option could be to use color groupings within a number of separate beds around the garden: blue, pink, and white; pale yellow, cream, and salmon shades; purple, magenta, and brown-purple shades; or maroon, red, orange, and deep yellow. Or you could adopt a temperature theme: "hot" colors, which include reds, yellows, and oranges, can look spectacular in a warm, sunny position; for a "cool" bed in a semishaded site, use plants with flowers in shades of blue, green, and white.

Plants for a cool bed in semi-shade

Agapanthus Headbourne Hybrids	*Euphorbia amygdaloides* var. *robbiae*	*Polemonium* 'Sapphire'
Alchemilla mollis	*Geranium* 'Johnson's Blue'	*Pulmonaria angustifolia* subsp. *azurea*
Anaphalis yedoensis	*Geum* 'Rubin'	*Scabiosa* 'Butterfly Blue'
Astrantia major	*Iris sibirica*	*Tradescantia* 'Osprey'
Centranthus ruber var. *coccineus*	*Liriope muscari*	*Yucca flaccida* 'Ivory'
Dicentra spectabilis 'Alba'	*Nepeta* 'Six Hills Giant'	

Geranium 'Johnson's Blue'

Plants for a hot bed in a warm, sunny position

Achillea filipendulina 'Gold Plate'	*Hemerocallis* 'Stella de Oro'	*Rudbeckia fulgida* var. *sullivanii* 'Goldsturm'
Bergenia 'Morgenrote'	*Incarvillea delavayi*	*Saponaria ocymoides*
Cosmos atrosanguineus	*Kniphofia caulescens*	*Schizostylis coccinea* 'Major'
Crocosmia masoniorum	*Ligularia* 'The Rocket'	*Sedum* 'Autumn Joy'
Dahlia 'Bishop of Llandaff'	*Oenothera missouriensis*	*Trollius* 'Orange Princess'
Dianthus 'Christopher'	*Penstemon* 'Garnet'	
	Potentilla 'Gibson's Scarlet'	

Rudbeckia fulgida

summer bedding

The whole idea of summer bedding is to create a loud, bold display to reflect the brightest, warmest season of the gardening year. With the help of a good seed catalog, it is remarkably easy to create a flowerbed that will provide color and interest all summer long. No special growing facilities are required. The main display can be produced from hardy annuals sown directly into the bed in mid- to late spring, or early summer in colder areas. More tender plants, such as half-hardy annuals, can be grown from seeds or cuttings raised on the kitchen windowsill.

MATERIALS & EQUIPMENT

garden rake and trowel

high-phosphate fertilizer

sand

plastic bottle

plant seeds (see page 26)

stakes and twine

Preparing the bed

1   The bed can be marked out into planned blocks before
sowing any seeds.

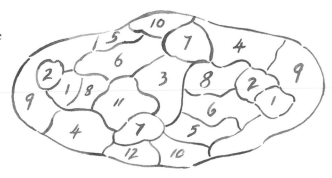

2   Prepare the ground thoroughly to give the seedlings a good start, and
rake the soil down to a fairly fine tilth, adding a high-phosphate fertilizer
at 1 ounce per square yard to encourage rapid root development.

3   The easiest way to mark the bed is to use dry sand. Slowly pour
the sand out of a plastic bottle, forming narrow lines to indicate the
intended margins of each group of plants. This will give a clear guide to
where to sow or plant each group. If the sizes of the blocks are not quite
right, you can rake the sand into the soil and mark the edges again.

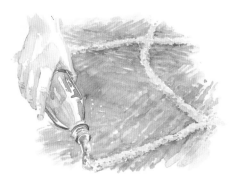

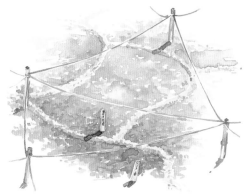

Sowing the hardy annuals

4   Sow the seeds into their respective segments, covering them lightly
with soil to prevent them from drying out. Label each group clearly.
Provide protection from birds if necessary by stringing lengths of twine
between short stakes.

5   At this stage, some segments should be left empty, with
no seed sown in them. These will accommodate the more
tender half-hardy annuals when they are planted out.

6   When the seedlings emerge, gradually thin them
out to give them plenty of room to grow.

KEY TO PLANTING SCHEME

1   *Solenostemon (Coleus) blumei*
(red-leaved form)

2   *Solenostemon (Coleus) blumei*
(cream-leaved form)

3   *Cosmos*

4   *Coreopsis*

5   *Gomphrena*

6   *Zinnia elegans*

7   *Gaillardia* × *grandiflora* 'Kobold'

8   *Verbena bonariensis*

9   *Scabiosa*

10 *Salvia viridis* 'Claryssa'

11 *Dahlia* (Collarette Series)

12 *Achillea ptarmatica*

Transplanting the half-hardy annuals

7   You can now add the more tender plants that you have raised from seed indoors (alternatively you can buy these as "starter plants" from a garden center). Start by digging a hole slightly larger than the plant's root system. Remove the young plant from its container and, holding the plant by its root ball, place it in the hole so it sits firmly on the bottom.

8   Using the trowel, pull the soil back into the hole around the plant, and firm gently into place. Immediately after planting, water around the base of the plant.

9   Test that the plant is securely in place by tugging a leaf gently upward. The leaf may tear, but the plant itself should not move.

10   As the bed comes into flower, fill any gaps with half-hardy annuals, or use dwarf annual climbers such as sweet peas to cover the ground. Regular deadheading will keep the display flowering for as long as possible.

planting vegetables and fruit

The main purpose of growing fruit and vegetables is to provide a constant supply of fresh and tasty produce, and there are things to do at most times of the year. Spring is a time of intense activity in the vegetable garden, and this is when the bulk of the salad crops are planted, as well as alpine strawberries, ready for eating once the weather has warmed up. However, as with any other time of the year, we see both ends of the cropping cycle in spring, with seeds being sown and plants raised, as well as harvesting of some overwintered crops. Summer is essentially the season for planning and growing. Many of the vegetables planted in the spring will be ready to harvest in summer, while those that mature through the fall, winter, and spring of the following year will need to be propagated and the young plants raised. Also in summer, other rapidly growing crops will need to be sown at regular, frequent intervals to make sure the continuity of supply is not broken. Fall is often seen as the quiet time in the vegetable garden, with harvesting being the main activity. However, some vegetables are tough enough to survive outdoors and need winter cold before they are ready to harvest.

crop rotation

For larger gardens it is a good idea to follow a crop rotation plan in your vegetable garden; this is a system used to move vegetable crops from one plot to another on a regular basis over a number of years, reducing the effect of both pests and disease, and balancing the nutrients that are taken from the soil. Simply divide the area to be planted into four plots, so that each one represents one of the rotational groups, then rotate the plots from year to year.

Root crops and greens	Brassicas	Legumes	Onions
Carrot	Cabbage	Greek bean	Garlic
Celery	Cauliflower	Lima bean	Leek
Parsnip	Radish	Peas	Onion
Pepper	Rutabaga	Snap bean	Scallion
Potato	Turnip	Snow pea	Shallot
Tomato			

bed systems

Where space is limited, a bed system can be used. This is a multi-row system where plants are grown close together and the distance between the rows is the same as the distance between the plants. The 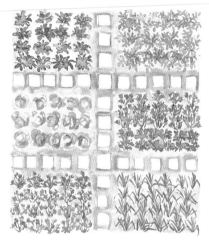 pathways between the beds are slightly wider than those on the row system, but because of the closer plant spacing, more plants can be grown. This arrangement makes the growth and shape of the vegetables more uniform. Weed control is made easier because the close spacing makes it difficult for weeds to establish themselves, and the soil structure is kept in a better condition, since there is far less soil compaction.

successional sowing

Quick-growing crops, especially the short-term salad vegetables, are the ones where gluts and shortages are the most likely to occur. But to a large extent, this situation can be avoided by careful planning, and by sowing batches of seed on a regular basis.

Timing
This can be hard to gauge for inexperienced gardeners, since many plants mature more rapidly in warmer weather. Figure out when to sow from the date you hope to harvest the crop, by counting back the number of weeks needed for the plants to grow. Sow the next batch of seed when the previous batch has germinated and emerged through the soil.

Vegetables for successional sowing	
Beans	Mesclun
Carrots	Radishes
Chinese cabbage	Scallions
Lettuces	Spinach

sowing vegetable seeds

1   Firm and roughly level an area of garden using a large-toothed rake. Add a base dressing of granular fertilizer and rake it into the soil.

2   Make a straight row using a stake with string. Use a hoe to make a seed trench to the depth specified on the seed packet.

3   Space the seeds evenly along the bottom of the trench, then rake loose soil over the top. Make sure the seeds are covered and pack the soil gently. Write the plant name on a label and insert it at the end of the row.

transplanting seedlings

After germination, seedlings are often too close together, and they will need to be moved (transplanted) to a different site where they will have plenty of space to grow and mature. The seedlings are usually ready for transplanting when they are about 3 inches high, each with four or five leaves.

1 Dig a planting hole large enough to accommodate the root system and, holding the plant by its stem or leaves, place it in the hole with the roots spread out evenly.

2 Using the trowel, pull the soil back into the hole around the seedling, leaving an indentation around the stem. Firm gently into place with your hands. Check to make sure the plant is secure by tugging a leaf upward. Water immediately after planting by filling the indentation around the base of the plant.

Seedlings for transplanting	
Artichoke	Fennel
Broccoli	Hot pepper
Brussels sprouts	Kale
Cabbage	Leeks
Chinese	Lettuce
Cauliflower	Sweet pepper
Collard greens	Swiss chard
Eggplant	Tomato

transplanting tender pot-grown seedlings

1 More tender vegetables, sown in pots, need to be transplanted into warm soil and grown through a sheet of black plastic, which will retain heat and moisture. Lay the plastic sheet over the soil and bury the edges.

2 Cut a cross in the plastic where the plant is to be inserted, fold back the flaps of plastic, and dig a planting hole large enough to accommodate the plant's root system. Work carefully to avoid tearing the plastic.

3 Turn the plant upside down and remove the pot. Holding the plant by the root ball, place it in the hole.

4 Pull the soil back into the hole around the plant, and firm gently into place, leaving a slight depression at the base of the stem.

5 Immediately after planting, water around the base of the plant. Fold the flaps of plastic back over the soil so they meet at the plant stem.

Pot-grown seedlings	
Corn	Pepper
Cucumber	Squash
Eggplant	Tomato

supporting vegetables

Tall-growing and climbing vegetables will need to be given some form of support as they develop in order to prevent the stems from becoming damaged or broken. The support will also help the plants bear the weight of the crop.

For green beans, use 8-foot stakes and erect them in two rows, at intervals of 24 inches. Join opposite stakes together at the top and place a horizontal bar over them. Sow the seeds at the base of each stake.

Once pea seedlings have emerged, plant pea sticks or twigs in the ground, either side of the seed trenches. Then, as the peas grow, they will attach themselves with tendrils to the sticks and gradually climb up them.

Taller-growing beans are better with some support. Insert stakes each end of the seed trenches, on each side of them, and tie string between them at a height of about 24 inches from the ground to enclose the plants.

pinching out

This is the process whereby the growing tip is removed by hand to encourage the formation of side shoots or flower buds—and thus fruit. Green beans and tomatoes benefit from this. Using your thumb and forefinger, pinch out the top buds once plants reach the required height, or for some beans once they are in full flower (this also deters aphids). If you want green bean plants to form a bush, pinch them out when 10 inches high.

protecting

Check plants regularly for pests and diseases. Remove any pests, such as slugs or caterpillars, and any damaged growth as soon as it becomes apparent, and treat where necessary (see "Pests and Diseases" on pages 240–41 for details). Another way to protect plants is to erect netting or other covers to deter predators (see "Summer Protection" on pages 238–39).

weeding

Weeds are particularly prevalent during summer, and you will need to check for them often, removing them as they occur to reduce competition for nutrients in the soil. Hand weeding is usually recommended for vegetable gardens, but other methods may also be appropriate. For more information on weed control, see pages 229–31.

sowing seeds outdoors

The vast majority of vegetables can be sown outdoors, directly into well-prepared beds, using either a broadcast (scattering) action or by sowing seeds in precise rows, as shown on page 30. (For more detailed information on sowing seeds, see pages 80–81.) After sowing, the seedlings will start to emerge above the soil level, and at this point they must be thinned out to the appropriate spacing to encourage proper development—but only when the first true leaf has appeared (ignore the initial seed leaves). This information is often found on the back of the seed packets. At this time, they may also need to be transplanted to their permanent beds (see page 81). If you are sowing seeds outdoors in the fall for harvesting in the spring of the new year, timing is critical. If you do it too early (say, in late summer), the young plants may become too mature and "bolt" in order to produce seed. If, however, you sow seed too late (say, in mid-fall), then the young plants may not have time to mature enough to survive the cold winter months. Judging the time to sow is largely a matter of experience, since it can vary by a week or two depending on the weather conditions in any given year. Your local county cooperative extension can tell you which crops and planting times are best in your area.

sowing seeds indoors

Some types of spring-sown seed need to be started off under protection, since the soil will be too cold for them to germinate successfully outdoors, and they also risk being damaged by any late frosts. Plant seeds in suitable seed trays or pots (see pages 86–87) and put them through a process of acclimatization, or hardening off (see page 34), once they have started to grow but before you plant them out.

Suitable seeds for outdoor sowing

Seed	Row spacing	Plant spacing
Beets	12 inches	4 inches
Beans	12 inches	9 inches
Cabbage—summer/fall	18 inches	12 inches
Cabbage—winter	18 inches	18 inches
Carrot	6 inches	4 inches
Cauliflower—early fall	12 inches	6 inches
Cauliflower—fall	12 inches	6 inches
Cauliflower—winter	12 inches	6 inches
Cauliflower—spring	12 inches	6 inches
Green bean	12 inches	3 inches
Kale	24 inches	18 inches
Kidney bean	12 inches	6 inches
Kohlrabi	12 inches	6 inches
Leek	4 inches	1 inch
Lettuce	12 inches	12 inches
Onion—scallion	4 inches	2 inches
Onion—seed	12 inches	4 inches
Parsnip	12 inches	6 inches
Pea	5 inches	5 inches
Radish	6 inches	1 inch
Rutabaga	15 inches	9 inches
Sprouting broccoli	14 inches	12 inches
Turnip	12 inches	6 inches

Suitable seeds for indoor sowing

Seed	Sowing density
Broccoli	40 seeds per tray
Brussels sprouts	40 seeds per tray
Cauliflower—summer	40 seeds per tray
Celeriac	40 seeds per tray
Celery	40 seeds per tray
Corn	1 seed per 3-inch pot
Cucumber	1 seed per 3-inch pot
Eggplant	1 seed per 3-inch pot
Pepper	1 seed per 3-inch pot
Squash	1 seed per 3-inch pot
Tomato	1 seed per 3-inch pot

hardening off

Plants raised indoors, or in a greenhouse, must be acclimatized for up to two weeks before transplanting. Bring them to a sheltered

area outdoors for a couple of hours each day, increasing this time daily. Alternatively, move them from the house or greenhouse into a cold frame or under cloches, and ventilate for a few hours each day, increasing the period until the frame is left open all day.

thinning and transplanting seedlings

Most seedlings need thinning out after germination to provide room for growth. If they need transplanting, do this while they are still young, when they are better able to recover. See page 81 for information on thinning and transplanting seedlings.

Transplanting in spring		
Plant	Row spacing	Plant spacing
Cauliflower—early summer	18 inches	24 inches
Cauliflower—summer	18 inches	24 inches
Celery	18 inches	24 inches
Garlic	8 inches	8 inches
Onion—sets	8 inches	6 inches
Potato	20 inches	12 inches

harvesting vegetables

The summer is a particularly busy time for the vegetable gardener, since many of the established plants will need constant attention to produce good crops. Routine-but-important tasks include training, staking, protecting, and weeding.

Salad crops

Salad crops—greens, radishes, and tomatoes—can be harvested throughout the summer. They should be picked as soon as they mature, so they do not deteriorate. This is especially true of lettuces, which will bolt if left in the ground too long.

Fall cauliflowers

Harvest fall cauliflowers from late summer until midwinter, when the covering leaves start to open and reveal the curd beneath. Remove the curd by cutting through the main stem with a sharp knife; leave a row of leaves around the curd to protect it from damage while it is being handled.

Onions

These are ready for harvesting when the leaves start turning yellow and the tops keel over. You can speed up this process by bending the tops over by hand. Lift the bulbs gently with a fork and leave them

to dry on a wire or wooden tray. Onions store well if they are hung in a cool, dry, frost-free place.

Podded vegetables

Where both the pod and its contents are intended to be eaten, start harvesting the crop once it is well developed and the seeds are just visible as slight swellings along the length of the pod.

Where just the seeds are to be eaten, they must be allowed to develop and swell, but you should harvest them before the pods start to change color and the seeds become hard and inedible.

harvesting spring vegetables

Fall-sown crops to harvest in spring are an option in mild-winter areas. Some are included in the table below; to learn what can be grown successfully in your area, check with a local expert. They can all be dug up out of the plot and either used when they are  fresh, or stored for later use. Most brassicas freeze well, and cabbages can be stored on a bed of straw under cover, such as a cold frame, or if you do not have one, a garden shed.

Spring-harvested vegetables	
Broccoli	Cauliflower—winter
Brussels sprouts	Kale
Cabbage—spring	Spinach

planting asparagus

Asparagus is a perennial and should not be planted with your other rotational crops—set aside a separate bed. Asparagus can be sown from seed in the spring, but it is easier to buy "crowns." Dig 12-inch-wide trenches, 8 inches deep and set the crowns 15 inches apart. Cover the roots with 1 inch of soil at first, adding more as the plants grow, until you reach the level of the surrounding soil.

planting alpine strawberries

There are several different types of strawberries. They can be broken up into three categories—summer-fruiting, perpetual-fruiting, and alpine. The first two types should be planted in late summer to produce crops the following summer. However, small, sweet-tasting alpine strawberries should be started in the spring. (Check the seed packet for additional details.)

Begin by sowing the seeds into trays of moist soil indoors, in early spring. Store the trays in a darkened room to aid germination (see pages 86–87 for information on sowing seeds indoors and transplanting).

After the last spring frost has passed, transplant the seedlings into beds outside. Topdress them with compost. They should produce fruit in the fall of the first season, or failing that, the following spring.

Varieties	
'Alpine Yellow'	
'Baron Solemacher'	
'Delicious'	

planting potatoes

Seed potatoes are easy to grow and need to be planted in the spring, in a frost-free environment, once the temperature has increased. The sprouts on the seed potatoes should be at least ¾ inch long for a high-yielding crop. Prepare your soil by digging in plenty of organic matter. Dig holes about 3 to 6 inches deep and plant the seed potatoes about 15 inches apart. Cover them with 1 inch of soil. In cooler climates, place a black plastic mulch over them, making holes in the cover for the emerging plants.

Varieties
'Ailsa'
'King Edward'
'Pink Fir Apple'
'Romano'
'Sante'

planting fall-sown onions

Onions are grown as annual plants, with the brown- or yellow-skinned cultivars being the most popular with gardeners. They are cool-temperature and even frost-tolerant plants, especially in the early stages of development, with low temperatures often promoting a better-quality crop. For this reason, many are raised from seed sown in the early fall, 1 inch apart, in holes ½ inch deep, with rows about 12 inches apart. The time of sowing is critical: if sown too early, seedlings become too mature and will begin producing seed; if sown too late, seedlings may not be mature enough to survive the winter. Sow once the weather turns cooler but before any frost.

Varieties
'Walla Walla Sweet'
(for South and
mild North)

planting garlic

This hardy vegetable with its strong flavor is surprisingly easy to grow. Plant garlic in the fall, or winter in warmer southern climates. The temperature must drop below 68°F in winter to promote good growth. Propagate bulbs by splitting them into cloves (individual segments), then push them base first into a light, deeply cultivated soil so that the pointed top of the clove is about 1 inch below the soil surface. Space them out at 7-inch intervals. As they develop, the bulbs work their way onto the soil surface.

planting early-summer cauliflowers

Use this method in colder areas. In early fall, treat the soil with a low-nitrogen fertilizer. Then sow seed into trays, and when seedlings have developed their first true leaf, prick them out and place in pots 3 x 3 inches of loam-based medium. Put them in a cold frame in the fall, ventilate on warm days, and water sparingly.

planting beans

Beans are rich in protein and provide nourishment to the soil in the form of nitrogen. In mild winter areas, beans can be planted in the fall. Plant in early spring in the North. Check with your local cooperative extension to be sure of planting times for your area. Start by placing the seeds in double rows set 9 inches apart, 2 inches deep and with 6-inch spaces between each seed. As a protective measure, cover the plants with cloches or floating mulches.

Varieties
'Aquadulce '
'Express'
'Imperial Green Long Pod'
'Jumbo'

planting blackberries

Blackberries come as bare-root plants and, because of their vigorous habit, they need to be supported on a fence or wall as they grow. Start by digging a shallow hole, large enough to spread out the roots of the plant. If using more than one plant, space them at least 10 feet apart. Place the plant in the hole, fill with soil, firm, and water. Prune the plant back to about 9 inches to encourage rapid growth.

Varieties
Summer-fruiting
'Arapaho'
'Chester'
'Hull'

Fall-fruiting
'Black Satin'
'John Innes'
'Oregon Thornless'
'Thornfree'
'Variegatus'

planting spring cabbage

If you live in the South, or a mild coastal area, cabbage seeds can be sown in a seedbed in August for an early spring crop. Move seedlings to the garden in cool fall temperatures so they can grow slowly over the winter. The young plants are ready to transplant when they have three true leaves. Pack the soil around the plants to prevent them drying out or being lifted by frozen soil.

Varieties
To find the best varieties for your area, contact your local cooperative extension.

planting raspberries

Raspberries can be planted throughout winter provided it remains reasonably dry; otherwise, plant in spring or early fall. Choose a well-drained site and erect posts in the ground 15 feet apart. Attach three wires to each post at 30-inch intervals—if you are planting more than one row, set the rows 6 feet apart. Dig trenches under the wires 6 inches wide and 8 inches deep. Place the plants in the trenches 18 inches apart, cover with soil, firm, and water.

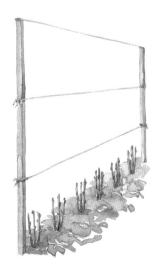

Varieties
Summer-fruiting
'Amity'
'Boyne'
'Heritage'

Fall-fruiting
'American Fallgold'
'Goldie'
'Honey Queen'

planting herbs

These aromatic plants, usually associated with culinary skills and food seasoning, also include a number of attractive ornamental garden plants that may be grown for their looks. Almost all herbs prefer to grow in a sunny position with a fertile, free-draining soil. The site must be cultivated deeply and cleared of all perennial weeds before any planting can be considered.

a culinary herb border

Traditionally, herb beds are arranged in a formal design to define the individual herbs and prevent plants becoming too straggly. Shrubby herbs are used as a framework planting to provide focal points and boundaries, into which the annual and biennial herbs are used as groundwork or filling. A modern approach is to lay out the paths in a symmetrical pattern to create beds, but soften this effect with informal plant-ings within the beds, which will provide color, aroma, leaf texture, and variations in height and shape.

Use the plan (right) and the chart below as a guide to planting your herbs, and see pages 17–22 for planting techniques.

Common herbs	Season of interest	Height
A Mint (*Mentha spicata*)	summer	1 to 3 feet
B Borage (*Borago officinalis*)	summer	1 to 3 feet
C Basil (*Ocimum basilicum*)	summer	6 to 18 inches
D Parsley (*Petroselinum crispum*)	summer	12 to 32 inches
E Fennel (*Foeniculum vulgare*)	summer	6 feet
F Coriander (*Coriandrum sativum*)	summer	20 inches
G Chives (*Allium schoenoprasum*)	summer	1 to 2 feet
H Thyme (*Thymus vulgaris*)	summer	6 to 9 inches
I Lavender (*Lavandula angustifolia*)	summer	1 to 2 feet
J Sage (*Salvia officinalis*)	summer	24 to 32 inches
K Bay (*Laurus nobilis*)	spring/summer	10 to 50 feet
L Rosemary (*Rosmarinus officinalis*)	spring/summer	5 feet
M Dill (*Anethum graveolens*)	summer	24 to 36 inches
N Horseradish (*Armoracia rusticana*)	summer	1 to 4 feet
O Angelica (*Angelica archangelica*)	summer	3 to 8 feet

Harvesting herbs

Harvest and dry your herbs to preserve their aromatic properties. Never wash them before drying, as they may start to rot. Tie short stems into bunches of eight to ten and hang them up in a warm, dry, and well-aired room until the leaves become crisp. Once dry, store the leaves in an airtight container.

Spring-harvested herbs	
Angelica	Lovage
Bay	Mint
Dill	Rosemary
Fennel	Sage
Horseradish	Thyme

making a hanging basket

Containers filled with plants are one of the most effective methods of linking the house and garden. They brighten up a dull corner or provide interest on a plain expanse of wall, adding color for a large part of the year. The project features a classic planting plan with a large fuchsia in the center, surrounded by smaller plants; however, you can use fewer varieties of plants in looser formation, as seen in the arrangement of impatiens, petunias, verbenas, and lobelias below, or a natural-looking display of nasturtiums, lobelias, and helichrysums.

MATERIALS & EQUIPMENT

wire basket, 16 inches in diameter with attached hanging chains

detergent, water, and large pot

galvanized angle bracket and screws

peat- or fiber-based lightweight potting soil and sheet moss

9 blue trailing lobelias (*L. erinus*)

1 large trailing fuchsia (*F.* 'Tom West')

3 Swan River daisies (*Brachyscome iberidifolia*)

3 white impatiens (*I.* New Guinea Group)

3 begonias

Preparing the soil for watering

1   Perhaps the most difficult problem to overcome with plants in hanging baskets is providing enough water to keep them growing well. There are effective solutions.

Mix 1 teaspoon of mild liquid dish soap into 2 gallons of water, and water the soil with this mixture before using it to fill the hanging basket. The soap forms a film over the soil particles and acts as a wetting agent, attracting water.

Alternatively, bury a small plastic bottle in the soil in the basket, and fill this each time you water—leave the cap slightly unscrewed so the water gradually seeps into the soil.

Securing the hanger

2   Choose the position for your basket carefully, taking into account both the display and ease of watering. Then attach a bracket to the wall, making sure it is secure and will support the weight of the finished basket.

3   While you are filling and planting the basket, place it on a clay pot, half full of soil, for support. Working will be much easier and the basket will not rock about.

Planting up

4   Start lining the basket by placing a 1-inch layer of sheet moss in the bottom half of the basket, patting it firmly against the frame. Hold the moss in place with handfuls of moist soil.

5   Add more soil up to the level of the moss and begin planting. Push the root balls of small trailing lobelias through the mesh of the basket from the outside and embed the roots in the soil.

6 Continue lining the basket with a 1-inch layer of sheet moss in the top half of the basket, patting it firmly against the frame of the basket. Add more soil up to the level of the moss, and continue planting all around the sides of the basket.

7 Now plant the top of the container, making sure it is as full as possible so the plants form a rounded shape when they are fully grown. Try to leave about 1 inch between the rim of the pot and the soil surface (this will give you enough room to water the basket). Plant the fuchsia in the center of the basket, packing the soil to anchor the plant.

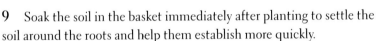

8 Position the Swan River daisies, begonias, and impatiens around the fuchsia, packing the soil firmly.

9 Soak the soil in the basket immediately after planting to settle the soil around the roots and help them establish more quickly.

10 After the basket has drained, lift the basket by its chains out of the pot and hang it in position.

planting hardy trees and shrubs

Trees and shrubs are easy to buy from nurseries and garden centers, and come in three forms: in a container, root-balled, or bare-rooted. They should be well balanced, with evenly spaced branches; this is particularly important for the main structural or framework branches. The plants should have no damaged or broken branches and stems, and should be free of all visible signs of pests and diseases. If possible, examine the root system of the plant and avoid plants with damaged roots, sucker growths, and containers where there are large populations of weeds in the soil.

plant forms

Container-grown   Root-balled   Bare-rooted

heeling in

If the transplanting site is not ready, plants can be placed in a site where they are "heeled in" (a form of temporary planting), though this should only be for a few days. Dig a shallow trench in a sheltered part of the garden and place the roots in the trench with the stems laid at an angle of about 45°. Refill the trench with soil and pack it gently, making sure all of the roots are covered with at least 8 inches of soil. This will protect the roots from damage until the intended permanent site is ready.

container-grown trees and shrubs

Plants grown in containers can be purchased and planted at any time of the year. For this reason container-grown plants are a convenient way of adding new or replacement plants to the garden.

Acer japonicum

Recommended plants

Beech	(*Fagus*)	Rose of Sharon	(*Hibiscus syriacus*)
Firethorn	(*Pyracantha*)	Tanyosho pine	(*Pinus densiflora* 'Umbraculifera')
Holly	(*Ilex*)		
Japanese maple	(*Acer japonicum*)	White cedar	(*Thuja occidentalis*)
Oak	(*Quercus*)		
Pfitzer juniper	(*Juniperus × media* 'Pfitzeriana')		

root-balled trees and shrubs

Plants bought as root-balled specimens are usually available in the fall and spring, but you can purchase them at other times of the year as well. When you buy your plant, check to make sure that the root ball is still tightly wrapped and unbroken.

Acer rubrum

Recommended plants

Callery pear	(*Pyrus calleryana*)	Japanese red pine	(*Pinus densiflora*)
Catawba rhododendron	(*Rhododendron catawbiense*)	Kentucky coffee tree	(*Gymnocladus dioica*)
		Manchurian lilac	(*Syringa patula*)
Common hornbeam	(*Carpinus betulus*)	Red maple	(*Acer rubrum*)
Eastern hemlock	(*Tsuga canadensis*)	Serbian spruce	(*Picea omorika*)
Green ash	(*Fraxinus pennsylvanica*)		

bare-rooted trees and shrubs

These bare-root plants will normally have some packing—such as straw—around their roots to protect them from drying out or frost. They are available when the plants are dormant and are planted in late fall or spring.

Malus prunifolia

Recommended plants

Amur cherry	(*Prunus maackii*)	Oak-leaved hydrangea	(*Hydrangea quercifolia*)
Aspen	(*Populus*)	Ohio buckeye	(*Aesculus glabra*)
Bridal wreath spirea	(*Spiraea* 'Arguta')	Red-twig dogwood	(*Cornus alba* 'Sibirica')
Crabapple	(*Malus*)	River birch	(*Betula nigra*)
Japanese barbery	(*Berberis thunbergii*)	Willow	(*Salix*)

planting a container-grown shrub

1   Using two stakes and a piece of string, mark the planting hole—a circle about twice the diameter of the root ball.

2   Dig the hole to at least twice the depth of the root ball, keeping the topsoil separate from the less-fertile subsoil.

3   Using a garden fork, break up the sides and bottom of the hole to allow the newly developed roots to penetrate the surrounding soil.

4   For tall shrubs it may be necessary to use a stake. Position it in the side of the hole and knock it into place until it is secure—it should reach the head of the shrub.

5   Add a layer of soil to the hole and pack it around the stake.

6   Take hold of the stem of the shrub and ease the plant out of its container, then tease out any enmeshed roots.

7   Return the shrub to the center of the hole, and use a bamboo stake or broom handle to check that the tree is at the correct level. Container-grown shrubs should be planted with the soil level in the container being level with that outside.

8   Start to backfill the hole with soil, spreading it evenly around the roots; hold the stem of the shrub steady while you do this. Fill the hole with layers of soil, finishing with the topsoil, and firm each layer with your heel until the hole has been filled up to its original level.

9   Anchor the shrub to the stake using a strap tie with a spacer, to keep the shrub and stake apart and prevent damage to the stem. The strap should be about 2 inches below the top of the stake.

10 Apply a topdressing of granular fertilizer to the soil around the base and scratch it into the top 2 inches. This will be gradually washed down into the root zone in time for new growth to start in the spring.

planting a root-balled conifer

1   This method is very similar to that of planting a container-grown plant (see left), but when you mark the planting hole, make it at least 2 or 3 times the diameter of the root ball.

2   Dig the hole, break up the sides, and add soil as for the container-grown shrub. Place the conifer in the center of the hole and tilt the plant gently to help remove the wrapping. Check that the top of the root ball is 1½ inches below soil level.

3   Backfill the hole with layers of soil, spreading it evenly around the root ball. Firm each layer with a heel, filling the hole to its original level.

4   Drive a support stake into the soil surrounding the planting hole at an angle of about 45°; this prevents breaking the root ball or damaging the root system. Point the top of the stake into the prevailing wind so the stem is tugging against the stake, and as the wind blows it drives the stake deeper into the ground. Tie the plant to the stake about 1 foot above ground level.

5   Apply a dressing of fertilizer around the base of the tree and mix it into the topsoil.

planting bare-root shrubs and trees

Some newly planted trees and large shrubs require staking and supporting until the roots are sufficiently anchored. Position the stake in the hole on the windward side, before planting, to avoid damaging the roots. Anchor the plant close to the base with a tie 6 to 8 inches above soil level. This will allow the roots to grow and establish, leaving the stem free to flex in the wind—helping it to thicken and develop.

Planting a bare-root rose

Roses are often offered for sale as bare-root plants. Exposing the roots means that they can become very dry. To overcome this, cover the roots in burlap and then soak them in a bucket of water for about half an hour before you begin planting. The best time to plant bare-root roses is in spring or fall if you live in a mild-winter area. With the soil still warm, they will establish very rapidly. They prefer rich soil and full sun. Make sure the "bud union," where the roots join the stem, is planted above the soil. However, in cold-winter areas, the bud union should be planted below the soil surface.

1 Dig the hole to at least twice the width of the plant's root system and deep enough to accommodate all of the roots. Using a garden fork, break up the soil in the bottom of the hole to allow the new roots to spread into the soil surrounding the planting hole.

2 Trim the roots of the plant with pruners to remove any broken or damaged pieces of root (damaged roots are often the sites where suckers develop).

3 Place the rose bush in the center of the hole and use a stake to check that the plant is at the correct level.

4 Backfill the hole with soil, spreading it evenly around the roots, and shake the stem of the tree to settle the soil between the roots and to remove any air pockets. Fill the hole with layers of soil to the original level, firming each layer with a heel.

5 Prune the rose to 3 to 4 inches from the bud union. Do this after planting, because the long shoots provide something to hold during planting. Apply a topdressing of granular fertilizer, mixing it into the top 2 inches. This will be washed down into the root zone.

transplanting

In addition to introducing new plants into the garden, there are times when it may be desirable or even necessary to move existing plants within the garden to make way for other plants, reduce competition between plants, or open up a particular vista. Careful planning and thorough preparation in advance of any move is essential.

Preparation

This process should begin in the early fall while the roots are still growing and the soil is still warm. This means that any roots that are pruned at this time will quickly heal and regrow. In the North, transplant in spring.

The first stage is to mark the intended size of the root ball, the diameter of which should be about one-third of the plant's height. Dig a trench outside this mark, 1 to 2 feet deep and one spade's width, cutting through any thick roots. Refill the trench with a mixture of soil, compost, and fertilizer to encourage plenty of new roots to form.

Lifting

The following fall dig a trench outside the one made the previous year, about 1 to 2 feet deep and the width of two spades. Cut under the root ball to sever any roots and separate it from the soil.

Rock the root ball to one side, place burlap or a tarp underneath, then rock it to the other side so that the ball is sitting on the burlap.

Bring the four corners of the wrapping together and tie in position. The plant is now ready to be moved to its new site.

Replanting

Position the root ball in a well-prepared planting hole. Untie and remove the wrapping (burlap can be left to rot in the ground). The transplanted plant should be at its original level. The hole around the root ball then needs to be refilled with soil and packed down.

Support taller plants with three angled stakes knocked into the surrounding soil, with guylines anchored two-thirds of the way up the main stem; attach sections of rubber hose to the rope to stop it rubbing against the bark. Finally, water and apply a mulch.

using trees and shrubs in containers

Growing trees and shrubs in containers is the ideal way for many gardeners to increase quickly the range of plants they grow, especially for those with only a little spare time, since there is no major soil preparation to be done. Fall and spring are the usual times for planting, but grown in containers, trees and shrubs will happily establish themselves in the summer, which is particularly useful for those wanting to create an instant display.

advantages of containers

There are many advantages to growing plants in containers, especially for those with small gardens, or even no garden at all. It can offer solutions to problems of space, soil, and climate, or provide a simple means of filling an unexpected gap in a bed. We usually think first of bedding plants as the planting material, but trees or shrubs combined with perennials and annuals create a permanent feature and a continual source of pleasure.

Dealing with lack of space
Plants in containers can be used to add interest to a small garden, because they can be moved from one site to another and so help vary the seasonal display. The use of containers is also a very effective way of restricting the growth or spread of very vigorous plants.

Gardens with no soil
It is quite feasible to grow plants outdoors without having a garden. Plants can easily be grown in containers and positioned on a terrace or balcony. Bay trees and thyme make excellent pot-grown herbs.

Adapting to different climates
In the North or areas that are susceptible to late-spring frosts, the growth rate of plants can be limited. By using containers, the plants can be moved to a more sheltered site or even taken indoors at certain times. This is very useful for pot-grown citrus fruits, such as lemons, which cannot survive freezing temperatures.

Different soil types
Some plants thrive only in certain soil conditions, but there are limits to how much you can modify the soil in your garden to suit. In some gardens the soil has a high lime content, which is difficult and expensive to adjust. This makes growing

plants that need acid soil, such as rhododendrons and camellias, impossible. The easy answer to this problem is to grow the plants you want in a container, in a specially formulated soil.

choosing containers

Containers are available in a wide variety of shapes, sizes, and materials, including concrete, clay, plastic, and wood. Alternatively, you can make your own, either from scratch or by giving a new lease on life to an object that started as something completely different (see the project on page 244).

Size and shape

While the final selection of a container may be down to personal choice, there are some practical considerations to be taken into account. Tall plants and climbing plants may need some form of support if they are to keep growing well. In this situation the dimensions of the container are particularly important; a deep container is necessary so that a stake can be driven into the soil. Also the shape of the container will have a bearing on how rapidly the soil will dry out. One with a narrow base and wide top exposes a large surface area of soil to the atmosphere and will therefore dry out more quickly than one with a narrow top.

Porous materials

Containers made from a porous material, such as terracotta or wood, often lose a good deal of water through their sides due to evaporation. To a large extent, this loss can be avoided by lining the inner walls of the container with plastic sheeting before potting begins. Do not line the base of the container as this may impede drainage and cause the compost to become waterlogged.

trees and shrubs suitable for growing in containers

Pinus mugo 'Winter Gold'

Climbers and wall shrubs

Actinidia kolomikta	Grape (*Vitis*)	Trumpet vine
Campsis × tagliabuana	*Jasminum nudiflorum*	(*Ceanothus* and *Clematis*)
Euonymus fortunei cultivars	Honeysuckle vine (*Lonicera × heckrottii*)	*Wisteria sinensis* (as a standard)

Conifers

Cryptomeria japonica	*Juniperus scopulorum* 'Skyrocket'	Mugo pine (*Pinus mugo*)
Cupressus macrocarpa cultivars		*Picea abies* 'Nidiformis'
English yew (*Taxus baccata*)	Korean fir (*Abies koreana*)	*Thuja occidentalis* cultivars

Berberis

Deciduous trees and shrubs

Berberis thunbergii cultivars	*Fuchsia magellanica*	Spirea (*Spiraea japonica*)
Buddleia alternifolia	Japanese maple (*Acer palmatum*)	Star magnolia (*Magnolia stellata*)
Cider gum (*Eucalyptus gunnii*)		
Dove tree (*Davidia involucrata*)	*Philadelphus* 'Belle Etoile'	*Viburnum carlesii*

Evergreen trees and shrubs

Box (*Buxus* cultivars)	*Cordyline australis*	Lavender (*Lavandula angustifolia*)
Brachyglottis (*Senecio*) 'Sunshine'	*Escallonia* 'Slieve Donard'	
	Eucalyptus	*Mahonia aquifolium*
Camellia	*Laurus nobilis*	Yucca (*Yucca filamentosa*)

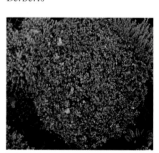

Buxus

planting a bare-root tree or shrub in a container

Growing trees or shrubs in containers is an excellent way of protecting tender species that may need to be brought inside over winter. It also provides the opportunity to plant trees in gardens with no soil, such as patio or roof gardens. Containers are also useful for plants that could not be grown in the garden, due to the soil being unsuitable. Rhododendrons and *Magnolia campbellii*, for instance, need acidic soil conditions.

1   Make sure the container has drainage holes and place a layer of pot shards over them to stop the soil from washing out. Add a layer of soil to cover them.

2   Make a small cross out of two 1½ x 1½ inch pieces of wood and wedge it horizontally in the pot, above the pot shards. Insert a stake and fasten it to the cross with strong wire.

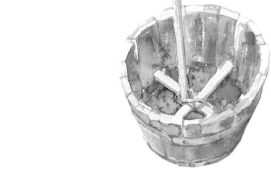

3   Place the tree in the container, spreading the roots evenly over the soil. Add soil around the roots. Shake the tree stem to settle the soil.

4   Fill the container with layers of soil, firming each layer, until the soil is 4 inches below the top rim. The plant should end up at the same level as it did in its previous location.

5   Make a second, larger cross out of wood and wedge it horizontally in the sides of the container, level with the soil. Fasten the stake to this cross with strong wire and cover with soil to hide the wood.

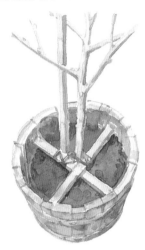

6   Anchor the tree to the stake using a strap tie and spacer to prevent the stake from damaging the stem. The strap tie should be 6 inches above the top of the container.

7   Using a saw, cut off any surplus stake about 2 inches above the tie—use a short stake, which will allow the stem to flex and bend in the wind, which then reduces the chances of the container blowing over in the wind.

8   Water the soil and apply a reflective mulch of light-colored stones or wood chips to prevent the soil from drying out.

a shrub bed for year-round interest

Summer offers the perfect opportunity to make plans for your bed, as you sit back and reflect on its present appearance and how you might like to change or improve it. Take inspiration from friends and neighbors, and visit as many show gardens as you can, so you can design the bed now, in preparation for planting in the fall. When choosing plants for a shrub bed, there are a number of factors to consider: the size and shape of the shrub, which colors and forms complement one another, the suitability of a plant for a certain site, and whether or not it grows well in your type of soil.

planning the bed

Perhaps one of the most interesting challenges for any gardener is to create a shrub bed that will offer something of interest throughout the year. This is not simply a matter of selecting a range of shrubs that flower at different times; it also involves siting individual plants so that they draw the eye to various parts of the bed.

1   *Chimonanthus praecox*
2   *Camellia japonica*
3   *Lonicera fragrantissima*
4   *Abeliophyllum distichum*
5   *Choisya ternata*
6   *Hydrangea macrophylla*
7   *Mahonia aquifolium* 'Apollo'
8   *Viburnum* × *bodnantense* 'Dawn'
9   Shrub rose
10 *Paeonia officinalis*
11 *Lavandula* 'Hidcote'
12 *Rosmarinus officinalis*
13 *Santolina pinnata* subsp. *neapolitana*
14 *Salvia officinalis*

Creating seasonal interest
One of the best ways to draw attention deep into a bed is to plant winter-flowering subjects at the rear, behind deciduous plants. The winter flowers can be seen through the deciduous shrubs, which will have no leaves on them at this time of year, but from mid-spring until mid-fall, when winter-flowering shrubs tend to be relatively uninteresting, the foliage of the deciduous plants will hide them from view.

Using scented plants
Siting scented shrubs close to paths and walks allows anyone nearby to appreciate their fragrance, whether it comes from the flowers or from aromatic foliage. Even if the shrub does not have a strong shape or spectacular color, its scent will add an extra delightful dimension to the bed.

planting for year-round interest

Spring

The new season is heralded by many small blooms in shades of cream, pink, white, and yellow. They are often highly visible, due to the lack of foliage so early in the year, and many are scented. Later on, more color is provided by the newly opening leaves.

Plants with good flower color	Plants with good foliage color
Daphne × burkwoodii	*Acer negundo* 'Flamingo'
Hamamelis mollis cultivars	*Berberis thunbergii* 'Atropurpurea Nana'
Kerria japonica 'Pleniflora'	*Elaeagnus* 'Gilt Edge'
Magnolia × soulangeana	*Mahonia fremontii*
Mahonia × media 'Charity'	*Pieris* 'Forest Flame'
Viburnum	

Magnolia × soulangeana

Summer

There is a huge choice of flowering shrubs for summer, and the plants can be combined to form a continuous display. Bear in mind that other colorful plants may offer stiff competition at this time, and interest can easily be diverted away from the shrub bed.

Plants with good flower color	Plants with good foliage color
Buddleia davidii	*Berberis thunbergii* 'Rose Glow'
Calycanthus occidentalis	*Catalpa bignonioides* 'Aurea'
Cistus ladanifer	*Cornus alternifolia* 'Argentea'
Rhododendron 'PJM'	*Physocarpus opulifolius* 'Diabolo'
Rosa 'Blanc Double de Coubert'	*Pyracantha* 'Mohave Silver'

Catalpa bignonioides 'Aurea'

Fall

A large number of shrubs grown for their spring or summer flowers provide a second season of interest in the fall. This is when many of the deciduous shrubs really come to the fore, with their dramatic displays of changing leaf colors. Many others produce attractive fruits, often remaining on the branches through winter and into spring.

Plants with good flower color	Plants with good foliage color	Plants with good fruit color
Ceanothus 'Burkwoodii'	*Acer palmatum*	*Ampelopsis brevipedunculata*
Clerodendrum trichotomum	*Cercidiphyllum japonicum*	*Ilex verticillata*
Convolvulus cneorum	*Cercis canadensis*	*Rosa rugosa*
Hibiscus syriacus cultivars	*Hydrangea quercifolia*	*Symphoricarpos orbiculatus*

Winter

Conifers and broad-leaved evergreens take center stage in winter, their attractive foliage often contrasting with orange, red, and yellow berries. There are also flowers at this time of year, with yellow predominating, and deciduous shrubs with brightly colored stems.

Plants with good flower color	Plants with good stem color
Camellia sasanqua cultivars	*Cornus alba*
Chimonanthus praecox	*Cornus stolonifera*
Jasminum nudiflorum	*Kerria japonica*
Mahonia × media cultivars	*Leycesteria formosa*
Rhododendron mucronulatum	*Rubus thibetanus*
Viburnum × bodnantense	*Salix sachalinensis* 'Sekka'

Cornus alba

making a tapestry hedge

A tapestry hedge is a selection of compatible plants with similar growth habits, used to create a hedge that provides a varied range of colors and textures. This type of hedge creates a feature in its own right, rather than being a backdrop for other ornamental plants, and the use of different plants often extends the season of interest. The most important aspect of a tapestry hedge is to choose plants (either deciduous or evergreen) that have very similar growth rates; otherwise, the most vigorous species will dominate the hedge to the detriment of its partners.

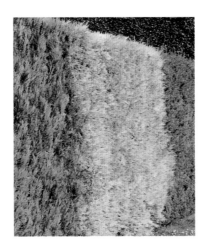

MATERIALS & EQUIPMENT

selection of suitable plants (see page 60)

organic matter, such as well-rotted manure or compost

garden twine

marker stakes

garden spade and fork

root fertilizer

pruners

1   Soil preparation

Hedges are permanent features in a garden, so it is essential to prepare the soil thoroughly. Start by marking a hedge line about 3 feet wide and double-dig the site (see page 253). Add copious quantities of organic matter as you dig. These cultivations should be carried out at least a month before planting. Be sure to dig out and remove all weeds, together with an application of a systemic weedkiller.

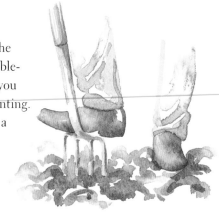

2   Plant selection

Choose three or four different plants from the examples below. Make sure they have a good root system, well-balanced stocky growth, and branches starting at soil level—this prevents gaps during early growth.

Common green beech (*Fagus sylvatica*)
Copper beech (*Fagus sylvatica purpurea*)
Holly (*Ilex aquifolium*)
Hornbeam (*Carpinus betulus*)
Purple barberry (*Berberis × ottawensis* 'Purpurea')
Quince (*Chaenomeles japonica*)
Yew (*Taxus baccata*)

3   Spacing

In most situations a single row of plants is enough to establish a good hedge, but on exposed sites or where a dense barrier is needed quickly, a double row of plants can be used. For most species (a single or double row), a spacing of 1½ to 2 feet between the plants is recommended. Where a double row is planted, the rows are 1 foot apart, with the plants staggered so they will knit together more rapidly. However, spacing should be determined by the shrub's eventual height and spread.

4   Planting a double row

Start by planning the positions for your plants. Mark the first line of the hedge with garden twine between two stakes, then insert more stakes along the length of the line at the correct spacings to indicate where the different plants are to be inserted.

5   Dig the first hole by the first marker stake; the hole should be large enough to accommodate the root system of the plant you have chosen. As you dig, keep the soil from the first hole in a wheelbarrow (this will be used later to fill in the last hole).

6 In order to get a good tapestry effect, mix the plants together and stand them in a bucket of water to prevent the roots from drying out. As the planting progresses, the hedge plants are simply pulled out at random and planted to give a mixed population within the hedge. For the first plant, place the root system against the side of the hole and spread out the roots; do not fill in the hole with soil at this stage.

7 Dig another hole by the second marker and place the soil in the first hole, covering the roots of the plant already inserted. Firm the soil in gently with a heel. Repeat this procedure down the entire length of the first row.

8 Now mark the second line of the hedge, as before, and insert stakes where the plants will go.

9 Start planting the second row, working back along the hedge line in the opposite direction from the first row. At the end of the row, the last hole is filled with the soil that was placed in the wheelbarrow in step 5.

10 Apply a dressing of fertilizer to the soil surface around the young plants and mix it into the top 2 inches.

11 Add a layer of organic matter 4 inches deep over the surface to act as a mulch, to retain moisture and suppress weeds.

12 Formative pruning

Pruning is essential to encourage even growth at the base and top of the hedge. Most hedges benefit from being cut back to two-thirds of their original height immediately after planting. At the same time, cut back any strong lateral branches by about half to encourage a dense, bushy habit.

planting climbers

Most climbers are purchased as container-grown plants. They can be planted at almost any time of the year, but planting in the spring offers a number of benefits. The soil is moist and starting to warm up as the days become longer and the sun warmer, providing the longest possible growing period in the new site and allowing plenty of time for the plant to establish successfully. Also, the risk of frost is diminishing, which is particularly important for plants that may not be fully hardy in your area.

Tropaeolum speciosum

Climbers for acid soil

Agapetes serpens

Asteranthera ovata

Chilean bellflower
  (*Lapageria rosea*)

Coral plant
  (*Berberidopsis corallina*)

Dusky coral pea
  (*Kennedia rubicunda*)

Flame nasturtium
  (*Tropaeolum speciosum*)

Herald's trumpet
  (*Beaumontia grandiflora*)

Holboellia coriacea

Lardizabala biternata

Mitraria coccinea

Mutisia ilicifolia

Passiflora caerulea

Climbers for alkaline soil

Actinidia kolomikta

American bittersweet
  (*Celastrus scandens*)

Blue passion flower
  (*Passiflora caerulea*)

Campsis

Chinese wisteria

  (*Wisteria sinensis*)

Chocolate vine
  (*Akebia quinata*)

Clematis

Climbing hydrangea
  (*Hydrangea anamola*
  subsp. *petiolaris*)

Confederate jasmine
  (*Trachelospermum
  jasminoides*)

Everlasting pea
  (*Lathyrus grandiflorus*)

Humulus lupulus 'Aureus'

Climbers for clay soil

Boston ivy
  (*Parthenocissus tricuspidata*)

Clematis
  "Large-flowered hybrids"

Dutchman's pipe
  (*Aristolochia durior*)

Everlasting pea
  (*Lathyrus latifolius*
  'White Pearl')

Golden hop
  (*Humulus lupulus* 'Aureus')

Rosa 'Zephirine Drouhin'

Trumpet vine
  (*Campsis radicans*)

Virginia creeper
  (*Parthenocissus quinquefolia*)

Wisteria sinensis

Ipomoea

Climbers for sandy soil

Coral plant
  (*Berberidopsis corallina*)

Dusky coral pea
  (*Kennedia rubicunda*)

Flame nasturtium
  (*Tropaeolum speciosum*)

Giant granadilla
  (*Passiflora quadrangularis*)

Glory pea (*Clianthus puniceus*)

Holboellia coriacea

Ipomoea

Merremia tuberosa

Mutisia ilicifolia

Paradise flower
  (*Solanum wendlandii*)

Vitis vinifera 'Purpurea'

planting a container-grown climber

1 Dig a planting hole large enough to accommodate the plant's root system, about 1 to 1½ feet away from the base of the support. Break up the soil in the base of the hole to encourage deep root penetration from the new plant.

2 Before planting, water the container thoroughly to moisten the plant's roots. Then holding the plant by its stem or leaves, gently remove it from the container and scrape away the top ½ inch of soil from the surface of the root ball and discard it (this layer will contain most weed seeds and moss, which may contaminate the planting site).

3 Tease out any roots that are curling around the bottom of the root ball and place the plant in the hole, leaning the top of the plant against the support.

4 Mix a dressing of slow-release fertilizer into the soil that will be used to refill the planting hole. Using a spade, pull the soil back in the hole around the plant and firm it gently into place. Cover the surface with soil, leaving a slight depression around the base of the stem.

5 After planting, water around the base of the plant with at least 2 gallons of water, to settle the soil around the plant's roots and encourage the roots to grow into the surrounding soil.

6 Untie the shoots from the bamboo stake, spread them out against the support frame, and tie them in position (even climbers with tendrils will need some help and guidance to start climbing in the right direction). Finally, cut out or reduce any surplus, weak, or badly damaged shoots.

routine care

Climbers are usually planted close to a wall and may lose a lot of moisture to the wall's foundations, so it is essential to replace this loss, especially after planting. Mulching is a useful method of reducing surface evaporation from the soil, particularly with clematis, which prefers a cool, moist root system. Scatter mulch evenly around  the root area at the base of the plant. It is especially important to make sure newly planted climbers are well watered. To help keep them supplied with water, a useful tip is to plant a section of plastic pipe close to the root system when the climber is planted. This pipe can be filled with water at regular intervals, and the water from the pipe will then seep out into the surrounding soil, encouraging deeper rooting.

making a rose arch

This rose arch provides the perfect opportunity for gardeners in mild-winter areas to plant hardy roses in the fall so they bloom the following summer. In cooler areas, take care over siting and selection. An arch creates a sense of mystery in the garden, inviting the viewer to walk through and discover another garden scene beyond. This rose arch, which is made from pretreated lumber, will become even more attractive as the wood slowly ages, while the red *Rosa* 'Excelsa' and *R.* 'Swan Lake' will bring color and fragrance to the garden during the summer months and into the early fall.

MATERIALS & EQUIPMENT

4 wooden upright posts, 8 feet tall and 4 inches in diameter

6 cross rails, 3 feet long and 4 inches in diameter

6 wooden diagonal braces, 5 feet long and 2 inches in diameter

2 main roof beams, 6½ feet long and 2 inches in diameter

3 roof cross rails, 3 feet long and 2 inches in diameter

2 wooden diagonal braces, 4½ feet long and 2 inches in diameter

4 wooden marker stakes and garden twine

4 metal post holders

level and square

screws, 4 inches long

nails, 4 inches long

sledgehammer

4 climbing or rambling roses

1   Rake the soil roughly level in the area intended for the structure. Mark the positions of the upright posts using the wooden pegs and garden twine, checking that the corners are at right angles with a square. The overall area should be 5 feet wide and 3 feet deep.

2   Insert a piece of scrap wood into the first metal post holder and drive into the ground using a sledgehammer until approximately ¾ to 1¼ inch of the holder is showing. Repeat the process for the remaining post holders to support the upright posts.

Making the side panels

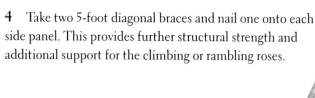

3   Make a side panel using three of the 3-foot horizontal cross rails and two 8-foot upright posts. Mark the position of the cross rails on the upright posts. Cut bird-mouth joints in the two upright posts and cut both ends of each cross rail into a chamfered point (see Glossary, page 259). Take each upright post in turn and insert the tip of the cross rails into the bird-mouth joints and nail together at an angle. Repeat this process for the other side panel.

4   Take two 5-foot diagonal braces and nail one onto each side panel. This provides further structural strength and additional support for the climbing or rambling roses.

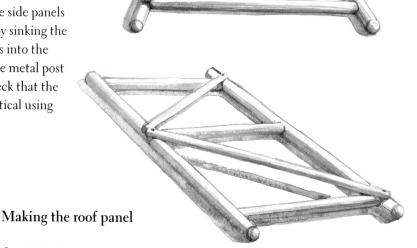

5   Erect the side panels of the arch by sinking the upright posts into the sockets of the metal post holders. Check that the posts are vertical using a level.

Making the roof panel

6   Make the roof panel in the same way as the side panels, using the two 6½-foot main roof beams and three 3-foot roof cross rails. Follow the instructions for making the side panels in step 3 to join the main roof beams to the cross rails. To provide further support, nail on two 4½-foot diagonal braces as in step 4.

7 Slot the horizontal roof panel inside the four upright posts and screw into position using 4-inch screws.

8 Fix four 5-foot diagonal braces to the top of the arch. Screw the lower ends onto the inside of the upright posts and the top ends onto the outside of the main roof beams.

9 Plant the four roses 6 inches from each upright post so the graft union is at soil level (in cold-winter areas, plant so the graft union is below the soil surface). Water in if the soil is dry and apply a slow-release fertilizer after planting.

10 Start training the roses over the arch in the next year using garden twine.

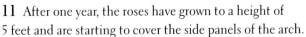

11 After one year, the roses have grown to a height of 5 feet and are starting to cover the side panels of the arch.

caring for new plants

The most important task to consider when caring for new plants is careful planning to conserve water, which helps the new plants to grow well in dry conditions. Incorporating well-rotted organic matter into the soil increases the moisture-holding capacity of the soil, and mulching to cover the soil surface with a layer of material is an ideal way of preventing surface evaporation from the soil. It is also vital that you keep an eye on the health of the plant, dealing with any pests or diseases at an early stage, before they can do any serious damage.

pests and diseases

Young plants and seedlings are particularly susceptible to pests and diseases, so you need to give them as much protection as possible in the early stages of growth. Healthy plants are better able to cope with invasion by pests and diseases, so the first stage in preventing lasting damage is to take the best possible care of your new plants. Always use clean containers and make sure you choose a suitable planting site with good spacing—the circulation of air helps growth and the health of the plant, as well as stopping the spread of pests and diseases from one plant to another. Also, water, prune, and remove any suspect leaves or branches as soon as they appear, before diseases can spread.

Diseases
The most common diseases are fungal, followed by bacterial. The most usual symptoms are discoloration and wilting or drying out of foliage and stems. Use either natural organic remedies or chemical controls to treat these problems.

Pests
On new plants the best method of control is simply to pick off the offending pests, such as slugs, snails, beetles, and caterpillars. Larger four-legged pests can be deterred by a chicken wire covering placed over your plants (see below).

watering seedlings

For seeds and seedlings, water must be in plentiful supply to enable germination and rapid development to take place. A moist seedbed is the best way to make sure that seeds will germinate quickly. If you water after sowing, the upper soil may dry out on a hot day, forming a thin crust that can prevent the seedlings from emerging after germination. Young plants being moved or transplanted often suffer from stress due to the disturbance, and this is even worse in dry soil. When watering seedlings, use only a light spray; first check that your water flow is steady (see below) and then pass the watering can gently over the plants (see bottom) to settle the moist soil around the roots.

competition

Any newly planted areas need all the help they can get to establish quickly—as well as feeding and watering these new plants, you also need to make sure they do not have to compete with weeds for supplies of food and water. Some form of weed control will need to be planned and implemented therefore, to reduce this competition. Chemicals that are usually sprayed onto the weeds can be used, but the best method is to tackle weeds by hand. For the most efficient weed elimination, use a hoe. The blade should penetrate no deeper than ½ inch into the ground, to reduce the loss of moisture from the soil and minimize soil disturbance, which encourages more weed seeds to germinate.

When hoeing out weeds between plants, sever the weeds at just below soil level, leaving the plants intact.

mulching

A mulch is basically a covering over the soil. In addition to retaining soil moisture, mulching also suppresses weeds. Problems can arise however, depending on the material used. Straw tends to harbor insects, such as vine weevil and flea beetles, as well as contain weed seeds. If you use an organic mulch, make sure it is at least 4 inches deep to be effective. A good alternative is to use a black plastic film mulch, which not only warms the soil (essential at the beginning of spring), but also is easy to apply and remove. As the plants grow, you can cut crosses in the plastic and gently pull through the developing stems and foliage.

shelter

Until they are established, many new plants benefit from shade and shelter to reduce water loss. To some extent, these problems can be overcome by hardening off the plants before they are planted out into the garden, but some form of protection for a few days can make a considerable difference in how quickly the plants start growing.

Plastic tunnels
These temporary structures are cheap, easily moved, and very versatile covers that can be laid over the crop (see below) and are ideal for vegetables that are grown in straight rows.

Fleece
For ornamental plants growing in beds, cut fleece into sheets or squares as an ideal frost protector and shade-giving cover. Fleece is more permeable to light and air than plastic film.

Plastic net
This finely meshed material can be placed directly over seedlings or plants and anchored with pegs (see below). It is good for filtering the wind and providing overall protection.

constructing
a rock garden

Rock gardens provide a unique growing environment for a wide range of
interesting and beautiful plants, and they can be the ideal solution to an awkward
slope where mowing or other forms of management and cultivation are difficult.
They are composed of rocks and free-draining soil arranged and built to imitate
a natural rocky outcrop, with plants arranged and planted between the rocks.

MATERIALS & EQUIPMENT

sandstone, limestone, or granite rocks

spade, rake, and trowel

coarse gravel and stones

gloves

wheelbarrow for moving large rocks

crowbar or strong rope

rock cress (*Arabis*), *Gentiana clusii*, pasque flower (*Pulsatilla halleri*),
Oxalis adenophylla, moss phlox (*Phlox subulata*), meadow saxifrage (*Saxifraga granulata*),
Sedum spathulifolium 'Purpureum', *Primula* 'Blossom', *Primula vulgaris*,
Lewisia tweedyi, yarrow (*Achillea*)

coarse grit mulch

Planning and preparing the site

1   Choose the site for your rock garden carefully. Alpines prefer a sunny environment with well-drained soil—preferably on a sloping bank. Once you have found a location, it is a good idea to plan your garden on paper, as this avoids having to reposition the rocks as you go.

2   Remove the topsoil to a depth of 6 inches over the site where the rock garden is to be built and stack it to one side for later use (if this soil is left at the base of the rock garden, it will be covered over and wasted).

3   Fill the excavated hole with coarse gravel and stones to improve drainage. Rake soil and old compost over the gravel to form a slight mound.

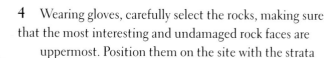

4   Wearing gloves, carefully select the rocks, making sure that the most interesting and undamaged rock faces are uppermost. Position them on the site with the strata running the same way and tilt them slightly to vary the overall height and allow any rain water to run off them. Drag large rocks into position and lift them onto the mound with a crowbar or strong rope.

5 Use the reserved topsoil to build up the area behind each of the rocks, as the layers of the mound are formed. Bury the rocks by up to one-third, or until they are steady and secure in the soil.

Planting

6 Before planting, water each plant thoroughly and allow the pot to drain for a couple of hours.

7 Using a trowel, excavate a hole large enough to accommodate the plant's root ball. Gently remove the plant from its container and lower the root ball into the prepared hole.

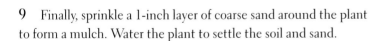

8 Fill in with soil and firm gently around the plant. Level the soil surface so it is just above the level of the root ball.

9 Finally, sprinkle a 1-inch layer of coarse sand around the plant to form a mulch. Water the plant to settle the soil and sand.

Care and maintenance

• Make sure there is always plenty of sharp sand or grit on the surface layer so the plants are always protected; this is usually done by topdressing in the spring, just after the plants have started to grow.

• Remove any dead leaves that accumulate on the rock garden, because once they have settled around the plants they tend to attract water and will eventually cause the plants to rot.

• Plants with hairy leaves are particularly susceptible to damage by wet conditions during the winter months or in early spring, and they may need to be protected by a sheet of plastic film.

propagation

One of the most satisfying aspects of gardening comes from the sheer satisfaction of producing your own plants, be it from cuttings, seeds, or any other method of propagation. Many of the techniques used are quite easy, often very little equipment is required, and the chances of success are high enough to make you want to keep trying. All methods of propagating plants other than from seed are known as vegetative propagation—this includes division and taking cuttings. The advantage of vegetative propagation is that you can be sure that any plant you reproduce vegetatively will be genetically identical to the parent plant. This is important in the propagation of especially fine forms of plants or variegated plants.

seed

Using seed is the most common and, in most cases, possibly the easiest method of propagating quickly a large number of plants. Seeds can vary greatly in appearance, germination requirements, germination performance, and growth rate. Some, such as birch (*Betula*), prefer cool, bright conditions for germination, while others, such as *Verbena*, can take up to three weeks to germinate and prefer warm, dark conditions.

tools and equipment

To begin propagation by seed, there are a few items you will need to add to your gardening equipment, if you do not already have them. You will need a number of different-sized pots—clay pots are the best kind, being both sturdy and deep. For seed trays, square or rectangular shapes will fit better on a shelf or window ledge. Use a multipurpose sterile soilless mix as a growing medium, because most garden soils will not be sterile.

A selection of clay pots is invaluable when you are potting seeds or seedlings.

Plastic seed trays can be bought with or without separate sections for your seeds. Use labels to avoid confusing seed types.

A rake and hoe can be used with pegs and string to keep your beds square and seed drills straight. Use a dibble (right) to make small planting holes.

Use a small watering can with a fine "rose" head so you don't wash away any soil and disturb the seeds.

Use a fine-mesh sifter to make sure the seed-starting medium contains no lumps or debris.

collecting seeds and bulbs

Although it is very convenient to buy seeds or bulbs in packs or bags, it is a relatively simple task—and much more satisfying—to gather them yourself from your own plants, or from those of a friend or neighbor. In some cases, especially with certain modern cultivars, plants raised from seed will not be exactly the same as the parent—but this can be part of the fun.

collecting seeds

With many plants, the seeds can be collected as they ripen but before they are dispersed from the fruit. It is much easier to pick the seed heads a day or two early and get all of the seed in one place; if you wait too long, you will find yourself having to pick up seeds from the ground, one by one. Observation is the key, because often the seed will mature before the fruit starts to split open. Once the pods begin to turn brown and you see the first signs of a split in the casing, the seed head and its contents can be collected.

Seed storage

1   Collect the seed heads complete with stalks, and remove any leaves or remaining petals. Place bunches of stalks, seed head first, into paper bags, and tie the neck with string. Label the bags.

2   Hang the bags in a cool, dry place. Shake them occasionally to release the seed. For smaller plants, lay the seed heads on trays lined with newspaper until the seed heads split open.

3   Carefully remove the seed heads and their stalks from the paper bags or tray. Hold the seed heads over sheets of paper and shake them until the seed falls out. Sift through with your fingers to take out bits of stalk or trash.

4   Place the cleaned seed in dry envelopes or other paper packs (not plastic bags) and seal them. Always take care to label the envelopes clearly, with the plant name and variety, the flower color (if appropriate), and the date.

5   Place the envelopes in a glass jar and seal the lid. Then put the jar in a cool, dry, dark place—this will help make sure the seed does not deteriorate. If they are properly dried and kept in the correct conditions, the seeds of most vegetables and flowering plants will survive from two to five years in storage.

Storage life of some seeds		
1–2 years	**3–5 years**	**5–10 years**
Callistephus chinensis	*Capsicum*	*Calendula*
Delphinium	*Centaurea candidissima*	*Cosmos*
Helichrysum monstrosus	*Phlox drummondii*	*Eschscholzia*
Iberis umbellata	Tomato	*Nigella*

pregermination treatment

A seed is a complete plant in embryo, but it is dormant. Before germination it may require some preliminary treatment. Seeds that have extremely hard coats, or display cold-temperature dormancy, will take a very long time to germinate unless you prepare them first. Stratification is a simple method of treating your seeds prior to sowing.

Stratification

This chilling technique, used for many seeds encased in fleshy fruits, such as hips and berries, allows the fleshy fruits to rot away but prevents seeds drying out. It is also used for seeds that germinate only in temperatures of 40°F or lower. When you have treated your seeds (see below), label the pot and stand it in a cool, moist spot in the garden. Periodically turn the mixture. Sow the seeds in the normal way the following spring.

1   Collect the hips or berries before they are fully ripe and place them in a paper bag.

2   Place broken sections of clay pot over the drainage hole at the base of your pot.

3   Place a 2-inch layer of sand or medium in the pot with a 2-inch layer of hips or berries over this.

4   Repeat this process until the pot is almost full, and finish with a layer of sand.

Some seeds that need stratification	
Aconite (*Aconitum*)	Maple (*Acer*)
Barberry (*Berberis*)	Primrose (*Primula*)
Birch (*Betula*)	*Sorbus*
Cotoneaster	*Viburnum*
Hornbeam (*Carpinus*)	

collecting stem bulbils

Some species of lily produce embryo bulbs, known as bulbils, in the angle created where the leaf joins the flower stem (the "leaf axil"). These immature bulbs can be collected after the flowers have died down and propagated to produce new plants that are identical to the parent. The bulbils are a dark green or blackish-purple color, and they form through the spring and summer months on the flower stem as it develops.

1   The best time to collect stem bulbils is when they are ripe, about three weeks after the flowers have died down. Simply pick them from the stem by hand—they should come away quite easily.

2   Sow the bulbils (just like seed) 1 inch apart in trays of seed-starting soil, positioning them so they sit just below the surface. Now place the trays in a cold frame and leave them for a year. The following fall, the young bulbs will be ready for planting out into a permanent site in the garden, although it will be a further two to three years before they produce any flowers.

Lilies that produce stem bulbils
Lilium bulbiferum
Lilium lancifolium
Lilium sargentiae
Lilium sulphureum

making a cold frame

Substantial structures, such as cold frames, are the best option for protection on
exposed sites where other materials and structures might be damaged or blown
away completely. A cold frame will not keep out all frost, but will reduce frost
penetration, especially if it is also lined with an additional insulation material,
such as fleece, clear plastic wrap, or bubble wrap. The best frames are those
made with good insulating materials—use wood for the sides and a single-
or double-glazed glass lid, either with or without a wooden frame.

MATERIALS & EQUIPMENT

lumber as follows:

48 feet x 4 x ¾ inch for body

118 x 2 x 2 inches for posts, two side supports, and central spar

48 x 3 x ½ inch for front of frame

3 x 1 x ½ inch slats for anchoring glass

48 x 2 x 1 inch for back rail

grooved lumber 144 x 2 x 1 inch with ⅜-inch-wide
and ½-inch-deep groove for frame sides and back

brass screws, 1 inch long

4 butt hinges

1 quart clear wood preservative

2 sheets horticultural glass, 21 x 24 x ¼ inch

Preparing the wood

1   Start by cutting the lumber into appropriate lengths for the body. For the front and back you need eight 4-foot-long boards: cut one of these in two along its length (use the other half for the sides). For the sides you need eight 2-foot-long boards, plus the extra length from the front and back, cut in two across its width.

Constructing the main body

3   Predrill three boards for the front at the short ends and screw them to two posts, with the excess at the top. Repeat this for the back panels using four and a half boards; place the narrow board at the top.

5   To create the sloping edge on the side panels, you need to saw a 6-inch diagonal "fall" from the back to the front of the main body of the box. Discard the excess wood.

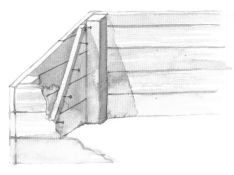

7   Cut the central spar to 24 inches and bevel the ends so that it fits exactly inside the box, positioned in the center and level with the top edge at both the front and the back. Predrill and screw it in place from the outside to form a supporting and strengthening bar.

2   Next cut out the wood for the four corner posts: the front two posts measure 13 inches and the back two posts measure 18 inches.

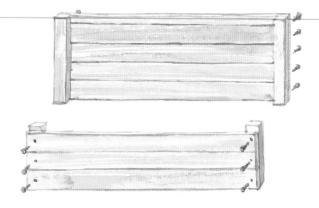

4   Now construct the sides, using four and a half boards for each side, and place the narrow boards at the top. Predrill and screw them to the front and back, covering the end grain of the front and back boards.

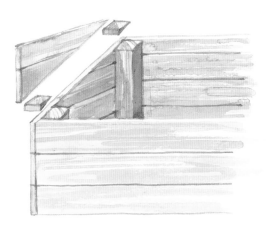

6   Now cut the two side supports, each measuring 16 inches, and nail them to the inside of both sides, positioning them at an angle so they join and secure the side boards (this keeps the sloping sections from flapping around).

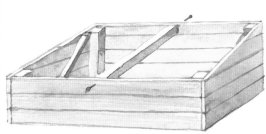

Constructing the frames

8 Cut the grooved wood into four 24-inch lengths for the sides and two 24-inch lengths for the back. Cut halving joints at the ends of all these pieces. Next cut the front-frame wood into two 24-inch sections.

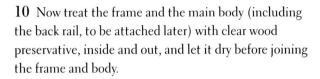

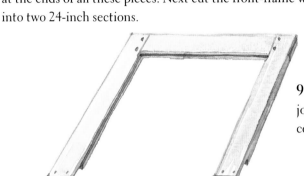

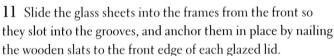

9 Assemble the frame back and sides by slotting the halving joints in place, then attach the front section. Secure all the corners with brass screws.

10 Now treat the frame and the main body (including the back rail, to be attached later) with clear wood preservative, inside and out, and let it dry before joining the frame and body.

11 Slide the glass sheets into the frames from the front so they slot into the grooves, and anchor them in place by nailing the wooden slats to the front edge of each glazed lid.

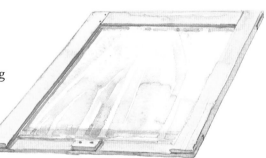

Assembling the box

12 Nail the back rail flush to the back edge of the body. Then place the glazed lids next to one another on top of the main body, butting the inside edge of the back rail. Screw two hinges to the top of each frame.

Using the frame

13 The completed frame is now ready for use. It can be used with the lid either fully closed or fully open. Also, sometimes it may be useful to have it half open in order to improve ventilation; to do this, hold the lid open by wedging a brick or similar object between the frame and the main body, along the front edge.

sowing seeds indoors

Many summer bedding plants are half-hardy annuals, and their seeds do not germinate in garden soil until early summer, because they need extra warmth. Other shrubs, trees, and vegetables are perfectly hardy once established, but are frost-tender during their seedling stage and benefit from protection or extra warmth early on. Some seeds also need light to germinate, whereas others must be kept in a dark room with no windows or where the windows have been blacked out.

seed sowing

1   Select a seed tray or pot and fill it to the rim with seed-starting soil. Firm gently until the soil is ½ inch below the rim of the seed tray, and for very fine seeds, such as begonia, sift an additional thin layer of fine medium over the surface.

2   For fine- and medium-size seeds, sow broadcast, half in one direction and the remainder in the opposite direction, to give even distribution over the tray.

3   For large seeds, create a regular pattern of holes in the medium (you can use a pencil or dibble for this task), and sow the seeds into the prepared holes.

4   Sift a thin layer of fine soil over the seeds and firm gently. For very fine seeds, simply press them into the surface rather than covering them with more soil.

5   Label and date the seeds. Insert the seed tray into another shallow tray of water and let the soil take up water by capillary action; let the surplus water drain away.

Seeds that require light to germinate	Seeds that require darkness to germinate
Ageratum	Amaranthus
Begonia	Cyclamen
Flowering tobacco (Nicotiana)	Love-in-a-mist (Nigella)
Impatiens	Nemesia
Lettuce (Lactuca sativa)	Onion (Allium)
Lobelia	Pansy (Viola)
Musk (Mimulus)	Phlox
Snapdragon (Antirrhinum)	Scorpion weed (Phacelia)

Allium

transplanting seedlings

As with seeds sown outdoors, the seedlings will need pricking out and transplanting. This is to remove weak seedlings and give the remainder more growing space.

1 Select a tray or pot of an appropriate size and fill it to the rim with potting soil. Firm gently until the soil is ½ inch below the rim of the tray.

2 Using a label or similar utensil, gently tease the seedlings out of the seed medium, making sure you do not damage the roots; hold the seedling up by pinching a leaf between your finger and thumb.

3 Make carefully positioned holes in the transplanting pot or tray with a dibble and lift the seedlings, placing them root first in the holes. Tap a small quantity of soil into each hole to cover the roots of the seedling.

4 When the pot or tray is completed, water the seedling to encourage growth. Use a watering can with a fine rose to settle the soil around the roots without damaging the delicate leaves.

5 Write the name of the plant and the date on a label (this will help you to predict the speed of growth in future years) and insert it in the side of the pot or tray, which should then be placed in a warm, shaded area to aid growth.

creating a suitable environment

As plants start to grow, they are at their most vulnerable and often need "intensive care," which means controlling temperature and moisture levels in an enclosed environment. However, warm humid conditions are an ideal breeding ground for fungal diseases, so make sure you remove any damaged or rotting plants to protect the others.

Protecting seedlings

In many situations, a plastic bag or sheet of plastic wrap over a plant pot or tray will provide an adequate propagation environment, suitable for many plants, but it is worth remembering that on hot sunny days, some form of shading will also be required to prevent sunscorch.

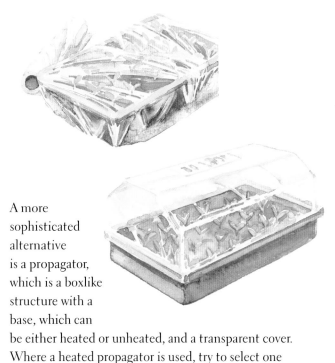

A more sophisticated alternative is a propagator, which is a boxlike structure with a base, which can be either heated or unheated, and a transparent cover. Where a heated propagator is used, try to select one with a thermostatically controlled heater so you can monitor the temperature accurately.

taking hardwood cuttings

This is an important method used by gardeners who want more of a favorite woody plant. These propagation techniques are not difficult to master, and little equipment is required. The formation of new root growth can be aided by the use of rooting hormones; these are available as powders (the base of the cutting is dipped into the powder and the excess gently tapped off) or liquids. Rooting hormones are available in a variety of different strengths—use one that is formulated for hardwood cuttings.

techniques

This technique is suitable for propagating a wide range of easy-to-grow deciduous trees and shrubs, and is probably the easiest and cheapest method of propagating plants from cuttings, since no special equipment or facilities are required. Hardwood cuttings are taken in late summer (North) or fall (in warmer areas), when the soil still retains summer warmth. Over the winter they will form a callus over the wound on the base, and start to root. As they develop in the spring, they will start to produce leaves and shoots.

1   Select healthy shoots of the current season's growth, which may be 9 to 24 inches long, and remove them from the parent plant with pruning shears (discard any thin or damaged shoots or those with obvious signs of pests or disease).

2   Using pruners, prepare the cuttings by trimming them into lengths of approximately 10 inches. Make a cut straight across the stem at the bottom of the cutting with sharp pruners. Make the second cut at the top of the cutting an angled one (straight for opposite buds); the length of the cutting is dictated by the position of the buds.

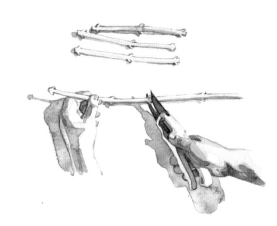

3   Prepare the ground by forking it over and roughly leveling it (there is no need for a fine seedbedlike tilth).

4   Cover the soil with a sheet of plastic and bury the edges in the soil (this reduces the need for irrigation, stops weeds, and encourages rooting below the surface).

5   Insert the tines of a garden fork vertically through the plastic into the soil below for about 6 inches—the holes are just the right diameter for most cuttings.

6 Gently push the cuttings, base first, through the holes in the plastic and into the soil to the right depth (see table, right). Shrub cuttings are inserted with the bottom two-thirds in the soil for a multistemmed plant. Tree cuttings are inserted until only the top bud shows, for a single-stemmed plant.

Multistemmed shrub or climber   *Single-stemmed tree*

7 Finish by pouring water into each hole containing a cutting (this firms in each cutting and builds up a reservoir of moisture beneath the plastic). After a hard frost, it may be necessary to firm the cuttings into position with your heel since the frost may loosen the cuttings in the soil. Over winter, the cuttings will start to root.

8 The following fall, slit the plastic mulch and dig up the one-year-old hardwood cuttings with a hand fork. The cuttings should now have roots and be ready for transplanting or potting.

Some plants that can be propagated by taking hardwood cuttings

Single-stemmed trees
(Plant with the top bud above soil level)

Black mulberry (*Morus nigra*)
Common laburnum (*Laburnum anagyroides*)
Cordyline
Dawn redwood (*Metasequoia glyptostroboides*)
Fig (*Ficus*)
London plane (*Platanus × hispanica*)
Mulberry (*Morus*)
White poplar (*Populus alba* 'Richardii')
Willow (*Salix*)

Multistemmed shrubs and climbers
(Plant the lower two-thirds below soil level)

Actinidia kolomikta
Bougainvillea
Box (*Buxus*)
Butterfly bush
   (*Buddleja davidii*)
Clematis montana
Currants (*Ribes*)
Elder (*Sambucus*)
Forsythia
Grape (*Vitis vinifera*)
Honeysuckle (*Lonicera*)
Mock orange (*Philadelphus*)
Potentilla

Red-twig dogwood
   (*Cornus alba*)
Russian vine
   (*Fallopia baldschuanica*)
Spiraea
Symphoricarpos
Tamarix
Viburnum
Weigela
Willow (*Salix*)

using a cold frame

In addition to rooting hardwood cuttings directly into a prepared bed outside, you can also use a cold frame (see page 82). Cuttings raised in this way, because of the protected environment, will usually root more quickly—typically by the following spring. Harden the rooted cuttings off (see page 20) before transplanting them into their final positions.

taking softwood cuttings

As the temperature rises and the days lengthen, many plants surge into growth, and it becomes too late for propagating by hardwood cuttings, as the plants are no longer dormant. For many broad-leaved evergreens and some conifers, it is too early to take semiripe cuttings, as the growth is not mature enough. However, many plants can be propagated by softwood cuttings when they are in active growth, and for a number of plants the most opportune time is the spring.

techniques

Select only strong vigorous shoots that are free from obvious signs of pests and disease, and avoid thin or weak shoots that originate from the center of the plant, since they tend to be too soft and sappy with long internodes (the spaces between the leaf joints).

1 Remove the shoots from the parent plant with a sharp knife or pruners.

2 If the stem of the cutting is more than 4 inches long, reduce it to a length of 3 to 4 inches by making a cut at a right angle to the stem with a sharp knife, cutting ⅛ inch above a leaf.

3 To keep the cuttings fresh and moist, place them in a small plastic bag with a few drops of water inside. Keep the bag closed, but do not seal it; excess moisture may cause the cutting to wilt.

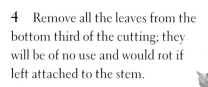

4 Remove all the leaves from the bottom third of the cutting; they will be of no use and would rot if left attached to the stem.

5 Dip the base of the cutting into a hormone rooting preparation—this consists of chemicals that are replicas of substances that occur naturally in the plants to promote rooting. Treat only the cut surface at the base, as contact with the rooting preparation may cause the soft juvenile bark on the cutting to rot. Tap off any surplus.

6 Select an appropriately sized tray or pot and fill it with potting soil. Remove a little from the top so it sits 1 inch from the top, but do *not* pack it down.

7   Push the cutting, base first, vertically into the free-draining soil, with the bottom third in the soil.

8   When all the cuttings have been inserted, water them gently to settle the medium around the base of the cuttings, without damaging them. The cuttings may appear very loose and floppy for a few days, but they will soon recover and look healthy, provided they are not allowed to dry out. Write the name of the plant and the date of propagation on a label and insert it at the end of the tray or pot.

9   Place the completed tray or group of pots in a shaded, damp environment to encourage the cuttings to root. With the more difficult subjects, a heated propagator can be used to help promote rapid callus development (healing) and root formation. Place the tray or pots under the cover and control the temperature to create the most suitable environment.

Some plants that can be increased by taking softwood cuttings

Alpines

Alpine pink
   (*Dianthus alpinus*)

Androsace lanuginosa

Horned violet
   (*Viola cornuta*)

Hypericum olympicum

Italian bellflower
   (*Campanula isophylla*)

Shrubs

Abelia × grandiflora

Caryopteris × clandonensis

Ceanothus gloriosus

Forsythia × intermedia

Hydrangea paniculata

Mock orange
   (*Philadelphus coronarius*)

Trees

Caucasian maple
   (*Acer cappadocicum*)

Erman's birch (*Betula ermanii*)

Eucryphia lucida

Goldenrain tree
   (*Koelreuteria paniculata*)

Indian bean tree
   (*Catalpa bignonioides*)

Smooth-leaved elm
   (*Ulmus minor*)

Perennials

Argyranthemum gracile
   'Chelsea girl'

Beardlip penstemon
   (*Penstemon barbatus*)

Bea balm (*Monarda didyma*)

Clover (*Trifolium*)

Delphinium bellamosum

Mallow (*Lavatera*)

Osteospermum 'Whirligig'

Ozark sundrops
   (*Oenothera macrocarpa*)

Verbena bonariensis

Climbers

Allamanda

Boston ivy
   (*Parthenocissus tricuspidata*)

Cape ivy (*Senecio macroglossus*)

Clematis montana

Climbing hydrangea
   (*Hydrangea petiolaris*)

Japanese wisteria
   (*Wisteria floribunda*)

Morning glory (*Ipomoea*)

Solanum

Thunbergia

Woodbine
   (*Lonicera periclymenum*)

Clematis montana

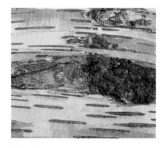

Betula ermanii

Monarda didyma
'Cambridge Scarlet'

taking semiripe cuttings

With higher temperatures and long hours of daylight in summer, many plants have a surge of growth and can be propagated by softwood cuttings well into the season. As this growth starts to harden and gradually matures, it becomes semiripe; this stage of development is ideal for taking cuttings of such plants as broad-leaved evergreens and some conifers. It is important to use only the best plants for propagation: the cuttings will be put under stress until they have rooted, and poor cuttings from poor plants will only deteriorate, never improve.

techniques

When collecting semiripe cuttings, choose only strong, vigorous shoots of the current season's growth. Do not select any thin or weak shoots, since they tend to be soft and sappy and usually rot. Discard any shoots showing signs of pests and disease.

1   Remove the shoots with hand pruners and place in a plastic bag with a little water to slow down wilting. Keep the bag closed but not sealed. Leave in a shady place if the cuttings are not to be potted immediately.

2   There are two types of semiripe cuttings, nodal and heel, the latter being more effective when propagating evergreens.

Nodal cuttings
If the shoot is more than 8 inches long, reduce it to 4 to 5 inches by making a cut straight across the stem with a sharp knife, ⅛ inch below a node or leaf joint. The positioning of the cut is important: the bark at the base of the cutting should be a light brown color, indicating that the semiripe wood is forming.

Heel cuttings
Pull a side shoot away from the main shoot, tearing it off with a strip of older wood (a heel) attached. The large wound stimulates root formation at the base of the cutting.

3   Strip away all leaves from the bottom third of the cutting. If you leave them in place, they will rot in the potting medium and encourage the cutting itself to rot.

4   Dip the cuttings into a hormone-rooting powder, to speed root formation. Treat only the exposed woody surface at the base of the cutting; if the hormone powder comes into contact with soft juvenile bark, it may cause the cutting to rot. Tap off any excess powder.

5 Insert the cuttings in a tray or pot of free-draining medium, or root them in a cold frame, planting the bottom third of the stem.

6 Water the cuttings gently to settle the soil. They may appear loose and floppy for a few days, but they should soon recover.

7 Write the name of the plant and the date of propagation on a label and insert it in the container or cold frame. Place pots or trays in a shaded, damp environment; keep the top of the cold frame shaded in very sunny weather. Check the soil regularly to make sure it does not dry out. Covering the cuttings with clear plastic will speed up callus development and root formation.

Some plants that can be increased by taking semiripe cuttings		
Climbers	**Conifers**	**Shrubs**
Akebia quinata	Chamaecyparis	Berberis (deciduous)
Fremontodendron	× cupressocyparis	Callicarpa bodinieri
Hedera	Cupressus	Ceanothus (evergreen)
Humulus lupulus 'Aureus'	Juniperus	Choisya ternata
Jasminum nudiflorum	Taxus	Escallonia 'Iveyi'
Passiflora	Thuja	Hydrangea
Trachelospermum	Thujopsis	Photinia 'Birmingham'
Wisteria	Tsuga	Viburnum carlesii

Passiflora caerulea

Thuja orientalis

Hydrangea 'Blue Wave'

division

This is one of the simplest and easiest propagation methods. As a basic technique, division involves separating one large plant into lots of smaller ones, or a number of small clumps, which are exact replicas of the parent plant. Although most plants are divided when they are dormant, there are some exceptions. Tall bearded iris and some primulas establish better if divided and transplanted soon after flowering, in early summer.

simple division

1   There are different methods of division, according to the type and size of your rootstock. "Simple" is the most basic technique and works well for young perennials. Start by carefully lifting the plant to be divided with a fork, making sure you do not damage the roots.

2   Shake the plant to remove as much loose soil as possible, and take off any debris, such as dead leaves and stalks. Then wash the plant thoroughly so that all the buds are clearly visible; this will reduce the amount of wear and damage on any knives and pruners being used.

Geranium × magnificum

Bergenia 'Beethoven'

Hosta

Some plants propagated by division		
Aster	Gentian (*Gentiana*)	Plantain lily (*Hosta*)
Astilbe	*Geranium*	Rhubarb (*Rheum*)
Bergenia	*Iris*	*Schizostylis*
Campion (*Lychnis*)	*Miscanthus*	*Stachys*
Daylily (*Hemerocallis*)	*Phormium*	Pansy (*Viola*)

simple division of fibrous-rooted plants

These plants often form a dense, overcrowded clump, which may become thick and matted with age. The performance of the clump will gradually deteriorate as those plants in the center become old and unproductive, often harboring disease. With this type of plant, and particularly members of the primula family, the problem is often one of getting some leverage on the plant without causing it too much damage. The leaves may be relatively soft and fleshy, and any attempt to pull the plant apart with your bare hands often results in two handfuls of leaves with the clump remaining intact.

1   Once the plant has been lifted and the soil washed off, force the prongs of two garden forks into the center of the clump so that they meet back to back. Apply pressure by levering the fork handles apart, then pulling them together again, until the clump starts to tease apart and splits in two.

2   This process can be repeated again and again, until the clumps are of the desired size. Each time, aim to inflict as little damage on the plant as you can. Before replanting, cut away old, dead, or diseased areas.

Gentiana sino-ornata

Alchemilla mollis

Pulsatilla vulgaris

Rock garden plants that can be increased by division

Achillea ageratifolia	Artemesia schmidtiana 'Nana'	Gentiana sino-ornata	Pulsatilla
Alchemilla mollis	Chiastophyllum oppositifolium	Golden creeping Jenny	Saxifraga apiculata
Allium sikkimense	Fairies' thimbles	(Lysimachia nummularia)	Sedum kamtschaticum
Antennaria dioica	(Campanula cochlearifolia)	Oxalis adenophylla	
Arenaria montana	Garden violet (Viola odorata)	Primula	

Persicaria bistorta 'Superba'

Pulmonaria 'Blue Ensign'

Epimedium × rubrum

simple division of irises

Rhizomatous plants such as irises have a thick fleshy modified stem, or rhizome, that spreads horizontally across the ground. These plants can be propagated by cutting the rhizome into sections, then replanting.

1   Using a garden fork, dig up the plant, easing it out of the ground with as much root as possible. Wash the soil off the clump so you can identify growth buds.

2   Cut the thick fleshy stem or rhizome into pieces with a sharp knife, making sure each section has a growth bud.

3   Check the rhizome pieces and discard any showing signs of decay or disease. Strip away any withered foliage, leaving four or five healthy leaves on each section. Trim these back to about 6 to 8 inches.

4   Dig a shallow planting hole large enough to accommodate the rhizome's root system. Then, holding the rhizome by its leaves, lay it flat on the floor of the hole and gently spread out the roots.

5   Pull the soil back into the hole around the plant and firm gently into place. Then water around the base of the plant to settle the soil and encourage the roots to grow.

planting

1   Divisions should be replanted at the same depth as the original plant, but any cultivars that are prone to crown rotting should be planted slightly above the soil level.

2   When replanting, make sure the roots are well spread out in the planting hole and the plant is firmed in. Water newly planted divisions thoroughly with a fungicidal solution to prevent rotting.

simple division of suckering shrubs

1 Dig carefully around the shrub with a fork and ease a section of root, with suckers on it, out of the ground.

2 Cut this section from the main plant with pruners or a sharp knife, making sure it has plenty of fibrous roots attached.

3 To prepare the root for planting, remove some of the leaves from the top section of the cutting.

4 Dig a planting hole for the shrub's root system, breaking up the soil in the base of the hole to encourage deep root penetration from the new plant.

5 Replant the sucker, firm in around the base, and water thoroughly.

division of snowdrops

1 After the flowers have died off, lift clumps up with a hand fork, making sure you do not damage the bulbs with the tines of the fork.

2 Shake all the loose soil from the roots and then carefully divide the clump, removing the individual bulbs.

3 Gently pull any bulblets away from the parent bulb —these can be replanted as well if they are in a good condition. These bulblets will simply take longer to develop than the main sections of the bulb, but they will eventually flower.

4 Replant the bulbs in the same depth of soil as they were originally planted. (See pages 12–13 for planting techniques.)

Suckering shrubs that can be increased by division

Amelanchier lamarkii

Berberis buxifolia

Bush honeysuckle
  (*Diervilla lonicera*)

Butcher's broom (*Ruscus aculeatus*)

Cassiope lycopodioides

Creeping dogwood
  (*Cornus canadensis*)

Euonymus fortunei

Gaultheria mucronata

Glory flower (*Clerodendrum bungei*)

Kerria japonica

Mahonia repens

Polygala chamaebuxus

Red chokeberry (*Aronia arbutifolia*)

Sarcococca humilis

Spiraea japonica

Sweetspire (*Itea virginica*)

bulb scaling

This technique is possibly the easiest method of propagation and is suitable for both lilies and fritillaries, the bulbs of which consist of clusters of scales attached to a basal plate. Very simply, the process involves encouraging the development of bulblets around the base of the scales; the bulblets can then be removed and potted to form new plants.

simple scaling

1   In late summer after flowering, as the stem begins to turn brown and dry, lift the bulbs from the ground and lay them in a seed tray to dry for two or three days. Then gently brush the soil from the outer scales of each bulb and remove the dead flower stem.

2   Detach the outer scales from the bulb by breaking them off at the point where they join the basal plate. You can remove up to 80% of the outer scales from the parent bulb, which will still grow if it is replanted.

3   Put the scales in a plastic bag and add fine-grade moist peat moss, so the bag contains equal proportions of peat and scales. Then add a small amount of fungicide, close the top, and turn the bag over several times to mix the contents evenly. Label the bag with the name and date, and put it in a warm, dark place, for about two to three months.

4   After this time each scale should have produced at least one small embryo bulb (there may be three or four). The bulblets will be about ¼ inch long, with tiny white fibrous roots growing from the base.

5   Plant each scale, complete with bulblets, in a 3-inch pot of medium, with just the tip of the old scale showing. Topdress with sand and place outdoors.

6   As the weather becomes warmer in the spring, new grasslike leaves will appear through the medium, growing from the bulblets. In the fall these young bulbs can be planted in the earth and may flower the following year.

twin scaling

Twin scaling is a modification of scaling often used on daffodils and narcissi. Its advantage is that it produces many more plants from a single bulb, although the bulb is destroyed in the process, and it does take longer for the new bulbs to reach flowering size.

1   Lift the dormant bulbs in midsummer, and lay them in a seed tray to dry for two or three days, before brushing the soil from the bulbs and removing the dead, dried roots.

2   Trim the top of the bulbs and peel away the outer brown scales from each one.

3   Using a clean, sharp knife, cut the bulb into eight equal segments. Cut from top to bottom, and make sure each segment has a piece of the bulb's basal plate attached.

4   Divide each segment into pairs of scales by peeling apart the layers and cutting them off, again making sure they have a piece of basal plate attached. Each segment should provide three or four twin-scale sections.

5   Soak the twin scales in a fungicide solution for 10 minutes, then leave them to drain on a wire rack for another 10 minutes.

6   Place the twin scales in a plastic bag containing moist vermiculite (equal parts vermiculite and bulb scales) and mix them together. Blow air into the bag, then seal it, and tie on a label with the plant's name and the date of propagation. Put the bag in a warm dark place for 12 to 14 weeks, turning it occasionally to keep the air moving.

7   By now, each twin scale should have formed at least one bulblet. Plant them into 2-inch pots of potting medium, then place them in a heated frame or greenhouse.

8   In spring the bulblets will produce grasslike leaves. As these die down, remove the bulblets from the scales. Repot in 2-inch pots and place in a cold frame. After another year, the young bulbs can be planted outdoors; they may flower three years later.

layering

This is ideal for plants that are difficult to root or would need specialized knowledge and facilities to make rooting cuttings a realistic proposition. This method of propagation simply involves the formation of new shoots on the new plant, before it is separated from the parent plant.

the principles of layering

A whole range of plants can be propagated by layering, provided the correct method is used, as some plants have slightly different requirements. There are three basic treatments: the first includes simple, serpentine, and tip layering, and involves planting a section of the stem into the soil; the second is stooling, which involves mounding soil over the stem; the third method, used for stiff or high branches, is referred to as air layering.

Simple layering

1   In spring, select a strong, healthy shoot of the previous season's growth and bend it down into a horizontal position. Two-thirds of the way along the shoot make a mark in the soil.

2   Where the soil has been marked, dig an oval-shaped hole about 6 inches deep using a trowel.

3   With a sharp knife, scrape away a 1-inch-long section of bark to cause a wound on the section of stem to be buried. Bring down the shoot into a horizontal position and gently bend it into the prepared hole.

4   Pin the stem into the bottom of the hole with an 8-inch-long "staple," made from heavy-gauge wire, to prevent the stem from springing back out of the ground.

5   Fill the hole with soil and firm gently. Water the soil if it becomes dry, to keep the stem moist and encourage roots to form.

6   In late winter, remove the soil and expose the roots that have formed at the base of each shoot. Cut off these new plants with as much root as possible and a small section of stem; they can now be replanted. (See "New Introductions" for planting.)

Serpentine layering

This is a variation on simple layering, used for vigorous plants with long flexible stems, such as clematis, climbing roses, and wisteria. This technique has the advantage that one stem can yield as many as five or six plants, rather than just the single plant per stem that is obtained by simple layering. Follow the method used for simple layering, but make several wounds on one long trailing shoot, in between buds, and pin down each wounded section leaving the section of stem in between exposed. Once they have rooted, cut each rooted section into an individual plant, ready for replanting.

Tip layering

Some plants layer themselves naturally; they have long arching stems that curve down to the ground, and where the tip of the stem comes into contact with the soil, adventitious roots form and grow into the soil. This can be encouraged by using a trowel to bury these tips about 6 inches deep into the soil so that a better root system is formed. In the late fall, sever the rooted layer from the parent plant, lift the new plants, and transplant them.

Stooling

Stooling, or mound layering, is often used to produce large numbers of plants, or rejuvenate an old plant that has become tall and straggly, or bare and open in the center.

1 In the early spring, cut down the plant to a height of about 2 inches and remove and discard all of the top growth.

2 The plant responds by producing lots of new shoots. When these reach 4 to 6 inches high, rake up soil to form a mound about 2 to 3 inches high around the base of each shoot.

3 Repeat this process in the summer when the shoots are 12 inches high, and again when they are 18 inches high; each time the bottom half of the shoots are covered until the mound is 8 inches high.

4 In late fall or early winter, carefully remove the mound of soil and expose the roots that will now have formed at the base of each individual shoot.

5 Once all of the soil has been removed, cut off these new plants with as much root as possible, but always leave a short stub of growth on the parent plant, since this is where the next layers will emerge. These plants can now be potted or planted in the garden.

Air layering

This method of propagation is used for plants with high branches or stiff shoots that cannot be lowered to soil level without breaking.

1 Choose a section of branch consisting of the current season's growth and clear any leaves or side shoots along a 6-inch stretch, starting 12 inches down from the shoot tip.

2 Make a diagonal cut on the underside of this bare section, about 2 inches long. Then bend the stem slightly to open the cut and wedge a small stone or twig into the cut to prevent the wound from healing.

3 Cut the bottom out of a plastic bag, pull it over the stem, and tie the bottom end 2 inches below the cut.

4 Fill the plastic sleeve with moist sphagnum moss, making sure there is plenty of moss around the cut. Fasten the top of the sleeve about 4 inches above the cut and then leave the sleeve on the plant for about 12 weeks to allow roots to form in the cut.

5 Finally, untie and carefully remove the plastic sleeve, making sure you do not damage the new roots. Cut off the shoot just below the newly formed root ball and replant it in a pot of medium (see "New Introductions" for planting). Keep the new plant well watered to encourage the roots to establish.

Plants suitable for simple, serpentine, and tip layering

Blackberry (*Rubus*)
Clematis
Corylopsis
Hazelnut (*Corylus*)
Honeysuckle (*Lonicera*)
Hops (*Humulus*)
Ivy (*Hedera*)
Winter jasmine (*Jasminum nudiflorum*)
Wisteria

Plants suitable for stooling

Apple (*Malus*)
Flowering currant (*Ribes*)
Heath (*Erica*)
Lavender (*Lavandula angustifolia*)
Smokebush (*Cotinus*)
Willow (*Salix*)
Wormwood (*Artemisia absinthium*)

Plants suitable for air layering

Bay laurel (*Laurus nobilis*)
Calico bush (*Kalmia latifolia*)
Chinese witch hazel (*Hamamelis mollis*)
Dove tree (*Davidia involucrata*)
English holly (*Ilex aquifolium*)

grafting

This method of propagation involves a process of joining separate plants together; the upper part or "scion" is a section of stem taken from the plant that is to be increased in numbers, and the lower part or "rootstock" needs to be as closely related to the scion as possible. Grafting is ideal for plants that are slow to root or will not produce roots of their own.

Whip and tongue grafting

It is possible to propagate most plants successfully with whip and tongue grafting, which is the most frequently used and simplest method of permanently interlocking two plants. All you need to begin is a good-quality sharp knife and a little practice.

1 To get the scion, select a healthy shoot of the current season's growth and remove it from the parent plant using pruning shears. Trim the scion into a 4- to 6-inch length; the top cut is made just above a bud and the bottom cut is made just below one.

2 Having chosen your rootstock, prepare it by making a flat cut across its top, 6 to 8 inches above soil level.

3 On the upper section of the rootstock, make a shallow upward slanting cut approximately 3 inches long on one side.

4 Starting 1 inch down this exposed side, make a shallow downward cut, about ½ inch deep, into the rootstock; this acts as a groove into which the scion is inserted.

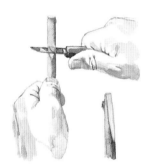

5 Now prepare the scion the same way by making a slanting cut approximately 3 inches long on the bottom section.

6 Then, 1 inch from the bottom of this cut, make another cut upward, ½ inch deep (try to avoid handling the cut surface), to match the groove in the rootstock.

7 Place the scion and rootstock together so the cut surfaces match and the grooves interlock.

8 Bind the graft with waterproof plastic tape. After 3 or 4 weeks when the stems start to heal together, slit the tape and let it split open.

seasonal pruning

It is very easy to dismiss pruning as a winter task, and for some plants winter is the main season for pruning, but for many others summer is the most appropriate time. Pruning includes the shaping and training of young plants, particularly those that must be clipped or trimmed into a predetermined shape or pattern, such as for topiary or formal hedges. Techniques used to control the growth habit of plants, such as training fruit trees into fans or espaliers, make it possible to grow them in a relatively confined space. Other forms of summer pruning include removing old, faded flowers, and stopping or pinching out the tip of a plant to form a large single bloom or a multistemmed plant with many clusters of small flowers.

shrubs

There are some shrubs, although not many, that will hardly ever need pruning; they are usually the broad-leaved evergreens, such as *Cotoneaster conspicuus*, *Ruscus aculeatus*, and *Sarcococca humilis*. However, by far the greater number of shrubs, if left to grow naturally, will eventually become overgrown and look unattractive, and will deteriorate over a period of time as the overall growth suffers and the health of the shrub declines. Careful, accurate pruning cuts will reduce the risk of damage to an absolute minimum. Cuts must be clean, with no crushing of the tissue or ragged edges. Always position the stem to be cut close to the base of the blade, where it can be firmly held; if the cut is made with the tip, the blades are liable to be strained or forced apart.

pruning techniques

Any cut you make should be in relation to a growth bud. This is important because rapid healing is greatly influenced by the close proximity of growth buds. Haphazard pruning is likely to result in the introduction of disease, die-back, and a bush with an unbalanced and unattractive appearance. Thin or twiggy branches can be safely pruned back using clippers.

As with any type of pruning, at any time of year, the position of the cut is important in promoting healthy growth. Even quite sturdy branches can be pruned with the right type of shears (see page 106); however, some people prefer to use a pruning knife. Choose a knife with a weight that suits you and a handle that comfortably fits in your hand. Handle pruning knives with care—they must be kept very sharp to do a proper job, so treat them with respect to avoid accidents.

positioning of pruning cuts

Select an appropriately placed bud facing the direction in which you want the new shoot to develop and cut the stems no more than ¼ inch immediately above a healthy bud or pair of buds. The direction of the cut varies depending on the arrangement of the buds (see below). As the shoot grows, it can be tied in to form part of a branch framework or be used to replace an old shoot. To encourage a plant to develop an open center, cut back to an outward-facing bud or shoot.

Alternate buds   *Opposite buds*

Drastic renovation

For the more drastic pruning in one season, cut away any weak shoots back to the stub and prune stonger growth to within 1 foot of soil level. If there are any suckers, cut them off at the base. Plants that have been grafted require special care; if the cuts are made below the graft union, the ornamental part of the plant may be cut away, leaving only sucker growths coming from the rootstock, particularly with some hybrid lilacs.

Pruning cuts should always be clean and go straight across the stem or branch.

Shrubs that tolerate drastic pruning

Barberry (*Berberis thunbergii*)
Common lilac (*Syringa vulgaris*)
Cotinus coggygria
Hazelnut (*Corylus*)
Spirea (*Spiraea japonica*)

Two-stage pruning

For the two-stage operation, in the first year remove all dead, diseased, and damaged wood and cut back half of the old stems to within 2 to 3 inches of ground level; always select the oldest growths for cutting back in the

first year, as they are most likely to harbor pests and diseases. When removing branches, lift them upward out of the shrub, as this does far less damage to the remaining stems that are to be kept for another year. The most efficient method is to cut through the largest (usually the oldest) stems with a small pruning saw and lift them clear of the plant. Cut large or tall stems into two or three sections to ease removal, particularly in windy weather. The following year, cut the remaining old stems and trim over-vigorous new growths.

pruning to create a barrier

If properly pruned, shrubs make attractive barriers in gardens. Barriers can be used to define a garden's boundaries, to divide the area up into a variety of "rooms," to direct the eye in specific directions, or to screen an unattractive feature, such as a storage area or compost heap. Aim to create, perhaps over a period of two years or more, thick growth right from the base of the shrub to provide a complete barrier.

Shrubs that are suitable for two-stage pruning

Beautybush (*Kolkwitzia*)
Deutzia
Dogwood (*Cornus alba*)
Firethorn (*Pyracantha*)
Flowering quince (*Chaenomeles*)
Mock orange (*Philadelphus*)
Wintersweet (*Chimonanthus*)

---

berries and fruits

The general rule with shrubs is that those that flower during the summer months are pruned immediately after the flowers have faded. However, there are exceptions to this, especially with those that provide additional seasonal interest in the form of attractive fall fruits, seed pods, and berries. These plants are often pruned in the late winter or early spring (once the danger of frost has passed), by cutting back the previous season's growth. This encourages the formation of flowering spurs for the new season.

Shrubs left unpruned for display

Barberry (*Berberis*)

Bladder senna (*Colutea*)

Chokeberry (*Aronia*)

Cotoneaster

Firethorn (*Pyracantha*)

Holly (*Ilex*)

Rosa rugosa

Sea buckthorn (*Hippophae*)

Snowberry (*Symphoricarpos*)

Pyracantha

Ilex

Rosa rugosa

Prunus

sap bleeding

Although, generally speaking, shrubs should ideally be pruned either after they have finished flowering or when they are dormant during the winter, some species will bleed large amounts of sap if they are pruned in the late winter or early spring, when the sap is rising. Examples include such common plants as some of the maples (*Acer*), some *Magnolia* species, and *Prunus*. To prevent this from happening, these shrubs should be left longer and pruned only when they are in full leaf. If you prune them in summer instead, when they are growing rapidly and the leaves have expanded, the leaves will search for any available moisture and will, as a result, draw the sap from the pruning wounds. This leaves them relatively dry and less susceptible to bleeding.

Shrubs that bleed and thus need summer pruning

Aesculus parviflora

Cherry (*Prunus*)

Japanese maple (*Acer japonica*, *Acer palmatum*)

Sophora

Star magnolia (*Magnolia stellata*)

---

pinching out

This is a useful technique often used for shaping a plant or getting it to produce lots of side shoots or branches. It is best employed when a shrub has almost reached the maximum height required. Pinching out involves removing the tip or growing point of each shoot. If this is done when the growth is soft and sappy, no pruning equipment is necessary, since the shoot tips can be pinched out between your finger and thumb. The trick is to pinch while the shrub is growing rapidly, since then the wound will heal quickly and so minimize the danger of disease entering the plant.

making a topiary design

Topiary is the clipping and training of plants into formal shapes. It involves early training followed by repeated restrictive pruning, the frequency of which depends on the intricacy of the design. The real secret to topiary is to prune little and often, constantly checking the plants and trimming them as necessary to form a dense, compact growth habit. Plants grown in pots are particularly convenient subjects for topiary, as they can be brought into the house and used for indoor display, although they will deteriorate rapidly if kept in for more than a few days.

MATERIALS & EQUIPMENT

pruners and hedge clippers

for a cone: 3 bamboo stakes, several yards of wire, and garden twine

for a spiral: thick wire

for a ball: bamboo stake and garden twine

suitable plants (see page 120)

Choosing a shape

Most topiary designs are easy to form if a template or framework is used. This will help to avoid accidents such as uneven trimming or, even worse, the removal of the wrong branch. For simple shapes, such as a cone or pyramid, stakes can be used for the framework; for more complex shapes, you may need a framework of wrought iron or chicken wire or a stake-and-wire structure. Other shapes, such as balls, can be clipped freestyle. Bear in mind that the more elaborate the design, the greater the maintenance required.

Selecting suitable plants

The plants that make good subjects for topiary must have certain characteristics for the growing and training to be successful. Those that respond well include plants with pliable growth that trains easily, a dense and compact growth habit, and attractive foliage.

Plants suitable for topiary
Aster bush (*Olearia nummulariifolia*)
Barberry (*Berberis*)
Bay laurel (*Laurus nobilis*)
Box (*Buxus*)
Boxleaf honeysuckle (*Lonicera nitida*)
Cotton lavender (*Santolina chamaecyparissus*)
False holly (*Osmanthus heterophyllus*)
Holly (*Ilex*)
Italian cypress (*Cupressus sempervirens*)
Jasmine box (*Phillyrea latifolia*)
Privet (*Ligustrum ovalifolium*)
Sagebrush (*Artemisia abrotanum*)
Yew (*Taxus*)

Making a topiary cone

1   In the first summer, cut back any long vigorous shoots that are spoiling the overall shape. The aim is to encourage the plant to grow as evenly as possible. Apply fertilizer if necessary to make sure the plant is growing strongly before clipping.

2   The following summer, make a framework of bamboo stakes and wire. Place the stakes over the plant, tie them together at the top, and wrap a few lengths of wire around them, spacing them evenly up to the top of the plant.

3   Shake all of the branches to encourage the longer ones to emerge through the stake-and-wire framework. Then, using a sharp pruner, clip the plant, removing any growth that extends beyond the frame.

4   When the clipping is finished, remove the framework. Next, cut back or pinch out the growing point by one-third to encourage the plant to produce side shoots and so become more bushy. This clipping and pinching will need to be repeated at least two or three times each year, depending on the plants used and their rate of growth.

Making a topiary spiral

1 A spiral can be achieved in two stages, but it will take several years to complete. First trim the plant as for a cone. Once it has reached the required height, wind a thick wire evenly around the cone to act as a guide.

2 Clipping from the bottom, remove some of the growth around the wire until a spiral channel is formed.

3 Once a definite spiral is visible, you can remove the wire. Clip new growth regularly to retain the shape.

Making a topiary ball

1 This shape can be achieved without the use of a template. In the first season, tie the main stem to a stake for support, then trim away the lower shoots.

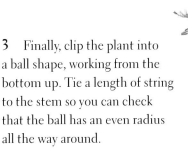

2 Cut back the growing tip by one-third once the plant reaches the required height. Trim the horizontal branches where necessary to encourage a dense, bushy habit.

3 Finally, clip the plant into a ball shape, working from the bottom up. Tie a length of string to the stem so you can check that the ball has an even radius all the way around.

Care and maintenance

• Do not clip topiary after late summer because soft young shoots are particularly vulnerable to frost damage in the late fall and winter.
• If any stems or branches become damaged or broken, they can be removed with pruners.
• To conceal any holes quickly, branches can be drawn together and tied with thin plastic-coated wire. The manipulated shoots will soon produce new shoots to fill the gaps, which can be trimmed as necessary as they develop.

climbing and wall plants

Pruning is essential to the successful cultivation of almost all established climbers. Without control, the plants eventually produce only a sparse display of flowers. More important, some of the most vigorous climbers may engulf neighboring plants or damage property. Climbers and wall shrubs are usually pruned, with the remaining strong, healthy stems being trained and tied to supports while they are still supple, to achieve the desired structure and appearance.

types of climber

Some climbers produce masses of long, slender shoots, which need to be tied in. Vigorous climbers can be left to grow freely, and *Wisteria* produces its best flower buds on horizontally trained branches. This demonstrates the importance of growth habits and basic cultivation in influencing the training and pruning of climbers and wall plants.

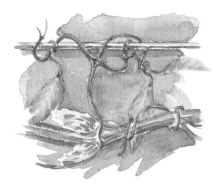

Twiners
Climbers, such as honeysuckle (*Lonicera*), *Clematis*, and *Wisteria*, climb on rapidly growing stems, supported by curling or twining tendrils, leafstalks, or stems. They may require additional support.

Scramblers and ramblers
These have rapidly growing stems, which clamber through other plants on hooked thorns or by rapid extension of lax shoots, as on firethorn (*Pyracantha*). They need a support structure on which to climb.

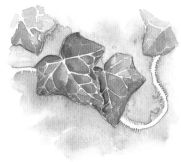

Climbing shrubs
Shrubs that are tender enough to need the protection of a wall or fence may grow next to a wall or fence, or be supported by it, depending on the plant grown. They will need to be tied in with garden twine.

Natural clingers
The natural clingers, such as ivy (*Hedera*) and Virginia creeper (*Parthenocissus*), support themselves by aerial roots or sucker pads. An additional support structure is not usually necessary for these climbers.

positioning of pruning cuts

The position of the cut and the technique employed are essential to improving the appearance of your plant and extending its life. Pruners will be strong enough, because most climbers have relatively thin stems. The best place to make the cut is just above a healthy bud, say $\frac{1}{16}$ to $\frac{1}{8}$ inch. If the cut is too close to the bud, you may damage it, and one placed too far from the bud will leave an exposed stem that will die back and encourage disease.

Decide on the direction you wish the climber to grow and cut at an angle in that same direction.

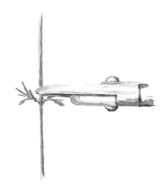

If the buds are opposite one another, make the cut so it goes straight across the stem.

methods of support

Climbers that have aerial roots or sucker pads will happily attach themselves to any structure. However, twiners, scramblers, and shrubs will need some assistance. Walls and fences can be covered in trellis, wire, or netting, and the plant can be attached either by weaving the stem around the support or by tying in the stems with garden twine.

A twiner in a wire frame support.

A scrambler tied to trellis.

formative pruning and training

Soon after planting, tie the strongest stems to the support system to achieve a well-balanced framework of shoots. This is essential with newly planted climbers, since the woody stems, which develop as the shoot becomes mature, cannot be bent into position without damaging them. As the plant grows, prune weak or damaged shoots, stems growing in the wrong direction, and crossing branches.

routine pruning

Climbing plants and wall shrubs are often used as decorative coverings for walls and fences, as garden dividers, or to give privacy or protection from winds around a patio or other seating area, so it is important to maintain their shape and health to promote vigorous new growths and attractive flowers. When you are dealing with established plants, the easiest approach is to prune them twice each year. The first pruning is carried out in the summer, when the new, long lateral growths are cut back to just above a growth bud. Framework shoots are then tied into position and left to twine around the supports provided for them (if they are self-supporting). The second pruning is carried out in late winter. At this time of year, all of the summer-pruned shoots should be cut back to form the spurs that will carry next year's flowers. Any secondary growths you find, which were formed as a result of the summer pruning, should also be reduced at this time, except with some evergreens, which require a different approach (see opposite). At any time of year, however, it is appropriate to remove damaged or diseased parts of the plant to maintain its health and vigor, or any stems that are growing in the wrong direction or causing an obstruction.

The lateral branches that will carry the next season's flowers should be shortened in the late winter to encourage new flowering shoots.

Always keep a check on, and prune, any tangled and crossing branches. This can be done at any time of year in order to maintain the plant's overall appearance and good health.

The dormant winter season is usually the best time of year to reposition ties. Make sure they are secure, but they should not be so tight that they rub against the stems or branches.

Pruning evergreens

Those evergreens that flower on the current season's growth are usually best pruned in the early spring—not in the summer, as is the more common practice with climbers. Remove all weak growth and damaged or congested stems, and retie the shoots securely, making sure they are not restricting or rubbing the branches.

Wall shrubs

Wall shrubs grown for their ornamental fruits, such as cotoneaster, produce most of their new growth in midsummer, after flowering. If left unpruned, these shoots will obscure the berries. In late summer, prune the new growths back to within 4 inches of the main stem. These short shoots then form spurs that will bear next year's flowers.

Climbers suitable for winter pruning	
Clematis texensis	Trumpet vine (*Campsis*)
Grape (*Vitis*)	Virginia creeper (*Parthenocissus*)
Oriental bittersweet (*Celastrus orbiculatus*)	Winter jasmine (*Jasminum nudiflorum*)
Pineapple broom (*Cytisus battandieri*)	*Wisteria sinensis*

Wisteria

Climbers suitable for spring pruning	
Cissus	*Distictis*
Clematis 'Barbara Jackman'	Dutchman's pipe (*Aristolochia*)
Clematis 'Carnaby'	Ivy (*Hedera*)
Clematis 'Duchess of Edinburgh'	Passion flower (*Passiflora*)
Clematis 'Henryi'	*Trachelospermum*
Clematis 'Nelly Moser'	

Escallonia

Climbers suitable for summer pruning	
Aristolochia	*Cotoneaster*
Billardiera	*Escallonia*
Campsis	*Hydrangea petiolaris*
Ceanothus	*Parthenocissus*
Chaenomeles	*Pyracantha*
Clematis armandii	*Thunbergia*
Clematis montana	*Wisteria*
Clerodendrum	

Clematis

renovation pruning

Neglected climbers soon become a tangled mass of woody stems that produce very few flowers, and when this happens, you have to decide whether or not the plant is worth trying to save. This can be done vigorously in one year, or, for climbers that are in particularly bad shape, it can be done over several years. A very badly diseased or infested plant may not be worth saving, and replacement is the only option.

Drastic renovation

If the plant is relatively healthy and vigorous, prune it very hard to rejuvenate it. Most deciduous climbers will tolerate being cut back close to the base or main framework of stems—the exception is evergreens, which are less suited to such drastic treatment. Cut the plant down to 12 inches with clean angled cuts, and as the new growth develops, train it over the support system. Less healthy plants will not survive this drastic treatment and should be renovated in stages.

Staged renovation

For staged renovation, remove the oldest stems (usually the darkest-colored bark) each year over a two- or three-year period. To avoid the new growth becoming tangled up in the old growth, in the first year cut down one half of the plant and train the new shoots into the open spaces. In the second year, the remainder of the old stems are cut away and replacements trained into the remaining space. Be prepared to wait for two or more years before the new growth is mature enough to produce flowers.

First year

Train and tie in the new shoots as they develop in response to renovation.

Second year

Untie new stems, cut out weak or damaged growth, and then re-tie the stems.

Climbers that tolerate renovation pruning

Clematis	Honeysuckle (*Lonicera*)
Coralvine (*Antigonon leptopus*)	Passion flower (*Passiflora*)
Glory bower (*Clerodendrum thomsoniae*)	Silver lace vine (*Polygonum aubertii*)
Golden trumpet (*Allamanda cathartica*)	Trumpet vine (*Campsis*)

wisteria

The vigorous habit of wisteria has deterred many gardeners from growing it, as they are not sure how to tackle the prolific growth to contain the stems and produce plenty of flowers. If pruning is carried out regularly, the task is fairly simple.

Pruning methods
In order to give an overview of the life cycle of wisteria, the illustrations below follow the pruning process from planting to maturity.

On planting
Attach support wires to a fence or wall. Tie the main stem to a stake, then cut the stem back to 2½ to 3 feet. Remove any side shoots.

First year—summer
Train long twining shoots into position to form a framework of branches. Cut back other shoots to 6 to 8 inches to encourage flower-bearing spurs to form.

First year—winter
In late winter, cut back the leading shoot and the lateral or side shoots until just three buds remain on each one. This will help in the formation of strong new branches.

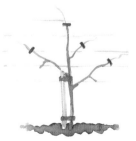

Second year—summer
Pinch out the tip of the leading shoot to the required height and cut back thin, spindly side shoots to encourage a bushy habit.

Second year—winter
To encourage the formation of spurs, which will eventually produce flowers, cut back the new lateral growth to two or three buds.

Third and subsequent years—summer
By now, only routine maintenance pruning will be needed. Keep the main framework branches in check by cutting back any over-long growths. Cut back lateral growth to 6 inches to encourage flowering spurs.

Third and subsequent years—winter
Cut back the flowering spurs to just two or three buds. This will stimulate growth and should guarantee the climber flowers well the following season. Check the ties on the main stem each year and replace if necessary.

installing a trellis

Installing a trellis panel on a wall is a good way of adding a new dimension to a garden by providing a support frame for climbers and wall shrubs, and making an expanse of plain wall interesting by covering all or part of it with attractive plants. The basic trellis offers many design possibilities and provides an almost limitless variety of garden options for the imaginative gardener. Attaching the trellis to hinges allows the whole structure to be removed, either to change the plant or to paint the surface behind.

MATERIALS & EQUIPMENT

4 feet x 2 x 1 inch sawed strip of wood

4 x 6½ feet hardwood trellis, with 4-inch-square grids

plastic wall anchors, to fit 3-inch screws

2 rustproof butt hinges

rustproof screws, 3 inches long

5 blocks of wood, 1 inch square, to act as spacers

screwdriver and hammer

electric drill; wood and masonry bits

chalk and measuring tape

hardy climber, such as *Campsis* or *Rosa*

organic matter, mulch, and garden ties

1 Making the trellis

Prepare the wooden strip by drilling five holes through it, spaced evenly from end to end.

2 Hold the strip horizontally against the wall, about 12 inches above ground level, and mark the wall with chalk to indicate the position of the holes.

3 Drill five holes into the wall where these marks are, using a masonry bit, and insert a wall anchor into each hole, tapping with a hammer so the top of the plug is flush with the surface of the wall.

4 Place the strip against the wall, lining up the holes with the wall anchors. Insert a screw through each hole in the strip, going into a wall anchor behind. Screw the strip securely to the wall using an electric drill or a screwdriver.

5 Take the hardwood trellis and lay it on the ground, then position the hinges along the bottom edge about 6 inches from the corners. Screw them into place.

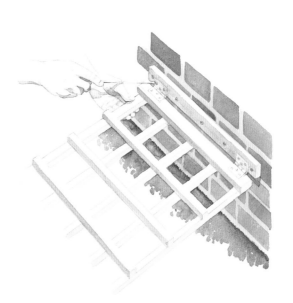

6 Leaving the top of the trellis on the ground, lift the base until it is level with the wall-mounted strip. Then position the hinges against the front edge of the strip and screw them into place.

7 Swing the trellis up on its hinges and mark the wall and trellis with chalk to indicate where holes will go in the corners and centers of the top horizontal strip. Also mark where holes will go in the middle of the side sections.

8 Drill the five marked holes, going all the way through the trellis frame. Then drill five corresponding holes in the wall using a masonry bit. Insert a wall anchor into each hole and tap them in, flush with the wall.

9 Spacers are now inserted so the stems can be trained between the trellis and the wall. Drill a hole through each wooden block and position them between the wall and trellis. Insert a screw through the hole in the trellis, going though the block and into the wall anchor. Screw securely in place.

10 Planting and training

Choose a hardy climber, such as *Campsis* or *Wisteria*. Remove the weeds from the soil and incorporate bulky organic matter. Dig a hole 1½ feet away from the wall, large enough to allow the roots to spread out.

11 Insert a stake and place the root ball in the hole, level with the surrounding soil. Fill the hole with soil, firm in, and tie the stem to the stake. Finally, water around the base and lay a mulch to deter weeds and keep the soil moist.

12 Using plastic ties or garden twine, tie the main stems to the trellis support system, spreading them out evenly so that as they grow, they will cover the main framework.

roses

In nature, the habit of most roses is to produce strong new stems from close to the base of the plant each year. As the new stems develop, they take priority for water and nutrients at the expense of the older existing stems, and these, in turn, gradually become weaker and eventually die of starvation. These old stems remain as deadwood before eventually rotting and falling to the ground. This is the closest plants come to being pruned in nature but illustrates that, in effect, the plant does prune itself.

rose types

The technique for pruning roses is relatively simple and only becomes complicated due to the different rose types and their varied growth rates and habits. Roses range from the low-growing patio and ground-cover types, which are often no more than 12 inches tall, to the very vigorous climbers, ramblers, and species roses, which can reach up to 30 to 45 feet tall. When and how you prune your rose can significantly affect the health of the plant, so it is important to follow the correct method. Some roses do not respond well to the recommended treatment for their particular classification, in which case you need to adapt your methods to suit their habit.

Modern bush—roses that grow in a cuplike shape and require more pruning than most species.

Shrub—a varied group, they tend to be mound-forming, but can also spread their branches quite widely.

Climbing—with long, strong shoots, these roses need to be trained and kept neat to create the best display.

general tasks

In order to keep all your roses growing and flowering well, or to improve their performance and the quality of the blooms, there are a number of tasks that should be tackled throughout the season, depending on the individual habit of your rose.

Disbudding

This is a technique that can be used to create fewer, but larger blooms on a rose bush. With most hybrid roses, as the new flower-bearing stem develops, the cluster of blooms will consist of one central bud and a number of small lateral buds. Snap off these lateral buds while they are still soft and sappy so that all of the plant's energies will be directed into the one remaining bloom, creating a much larger individual flower.

Deadheading

After flowering, dead rose blooms may remain on the plant for several months, and in this situation the plant will divert a good deal of energy into producing seed. Once this process starts, the plant gradually stops producing flowers altogether. A common mistake is to remove the flower with a length of stem bearing four or five leaves; removing the leaves is unnecessary and only a small section of stem, about 4 inches long, should be cut off with the dead bloom.

Sucker removal

A very important pruning task in the summer is removing suckers from roses. You can usually identify a sucker by its leaves. With most rose cultivars, the leaf consists of 5 to 7 leaflets, but suckers have leaves with 7 to 11 leaflets, each ending with a sharp point, and they are usually a much paler green than those on the rest of the plant.

1   Using a trowel, carefully dig the soil from around the base of the sucker, to the point where it is attached to the parent plant.

2   Wearing a thick leather glove to protect your hand from the thorns, grip the sucker firmly, just above the point where it is growing from the root of the parent.

3   Tear the sucker free from the parent plant and trim any loose bark on the parent with a sharp knife. Discard the sucker and replace the soil around the base of the plant.

Standard roses often produce suckers above ground, on the stem, in addition to those originating from the roots, and these may compete with the top growth and eventually take over. Wearing thick leather gloves, snap off the sucker growths where they are attached to the main stem or "leg" of the plant. Do this while the suckers are still soft and sappy.

shrub roses

This category includes modern shrubs, old garden, and species roses. These flower on old wood and need to be pruned only when they become untidy or to remove dead, diseased, or damaged wood; the best time to prune is after flowering. The main task is to remove the oldest stems just after the leaves have started to drop, usually in early fall. Due to its dense growth, this is one of the few times when you can see into the center of the plant, which provides an opportunity to get rid of diseased or damaged wood that may have an adverse effect on growth the following season. The drawback is that plants grown for their ornamental hips may have their overall display spoiled as a result.

rambling roses

These will flower quite satisfactorily for a number of years without any regular pruning, but they will eventually become a tangled mass of overcrowded, unmanageable shoots, prone to attack by pests and diseases, if they are neglected completely. The best time to prune is in the late summer, after the single flush of flowers is over.

Pruning cuts

As with all types of rose, you need to use clean, sharp clippers or a pruning knife to prevent ragged edges on the plant that may then become susceptible to invasion by pests and diseases. Make each cut at an angle, ¼ inch from an outward-facing bud. This helps keep the center of the plant open. Make sure to cut back into healthy white wood.

Routine pruning

Start by removing any dead, damaged, or diseased shoots, before cutting out about a quarter to a third of the oldest shoots; the aim is to leave only young, vigorous stems that are no more than two years old. Any side shoots should be cut back to two or three buds, from which many of the next year's flowers will originate.

Rosa 'Constance Spry'

Shrub roses	
Rosa 'Autumn Sunset'	
Rosa 'Canary Bird'	
Rosa 'Canterbury'	
Rosa 'Fountain'	

Rambling roses	
Rosa 'Albéric Barbier'	*Rosa* 'Rambling Rector'
Rosa 'Albertine'	*Rosa* 'Sanders' White'
Rosa 'Complicata'	*Rosa* 'Silver Moon'
Rosa 'Emily Gray'	*Rosa* 'Veilchenblau'
Rosa 'Goldfinch'	*Rosa* 'Wedding Day'

climbing roses

Climbing roses flower on the current season's growth and are repeat flowering. In the first and second years after planting, do not prune climbing roses, except to remove any dead, diseased, damaged, or weak growth. Then prune only if necessary. Never prune climbing sports of bush roses in the first two years, since they may revert to bush form.

Renewal pruning

Occasional renewal pruning may be necessary if the base of the rose becomes bare. Cut out several of the older, main shoots to within 6 inches or so of ground level, to encourage strong new shoots to develop and replace the older growths. Repeat this process in subsequent years, as required.

Begin training as soon as the new shoots are long enough to reach their supports. Training them sideways along horizontal supports will encourage flowering.

Many of these will produce flowers from the base of the plant without special training. The strong main shoots can be left unpruned unless they are getting too long, in which case shorten them as appropriate. Otherwise, simply shorten the side shoots.

Climbing roses	
Rosa 'Aloha'	*Rosa* 'New Dawn'
Rosa 'Altissimo'	*Rosa* 'Rosy Mantle'
Rosa 'Dublin Bay'	*Rosa* 'Royal Gold'
Rosa 'Elegance'	*Rosa* 'Summer Wine'
Rosa 'Handel'	*Rosa* 'Warm Welcome'
Rosa 'Meg'	

Rosa 'Pink Perpetue'

Rosa 'Madame Caroline Testout'

when to prune

How and when a particular type of hedge is pruned depends largely on the type of shrub involved and partly on the function of the hedge—as a backdrop for other ornamental plants in the garden, for example, or to provide privacy from neighboring properties, or to act as a visual stop and so prevent the eye from taking in all of a small garden at a single glance. As a general rule, the best time to prune is soon after flowering has finished. At this time, you should remove only the flower-bearing shoots. However, some flowering hedges and screens have more than a single season of interest. Plants such as firethorn (*Pyracantha*) or *Rosa rugosa* produce attractive berries or hips after the flowers have faded and should not be pruned until after the fruits have finished their display. Plants that require pruning in spring should generally be left until any danger of hard frosts has finished, but if the hedge is used by birds for nesting purposes, try to complete pruning before nest-building begins.

best tools to use

Broad-leaved evergreens, such as laurel (*Prunus laurocerasus*), should be cut with pruners for accuracy, so that only whole leaves are removed. Depending on the size and height of your hedge, this can be a time-consuming task, but any leaves that are cut in half develop a brown line where the cells have been damaged, and these "half leaves" slowly turn yellow and die. All other types of hedge can be clipped with a pair of hedge clippers. For very large hedges, electric hedge trimmers are a boon.

formal hedges

Evergreen hedges	Ideal maximum height	Best times for clipping
Box (*Buxus sempervirens*)	12–24 inches	3 x but not in winter
Elaeagnus × ebbingei	5–10 feet	1 x mid- to late summer
Firethorn (*Pyracantha*)	6½–10 feet	2 x after flowering and in fall, but avoid berries
Griselinia littoralis	4–10 feet	2 x late spring/summer
Holly (*Ilex aquifolium*)	6½–13 feet	1 x late summer
Laurel (*Prunus laurocerasus*)	4–10 feet	1 x mid to late summer
Leyland cypress (× *Cupressocyparis leylandii*)	6½–20 feet	3 x but not in winter
Lonicera nitida	3–4 feet	3 x but not in winter
Privet (*Ligustrum*)	5–10 feet	3 x but not in winter
Thuja occidentalis	6–10 feet	1 x spring
Western red cedar (*Thuja plicata*)	5–13 feet	2 x spring/early fall
Yew (*Taxus baccata*)	4–20 feet	2 x summer/fall
Deciduous hedges		
Barberry (*Berberis thunbergii*)	2–4 feet	1 x in summer
Beech (*Fagus*)	5–20 feet	1 x late summer
Hawthorn (*Crataegus monogyna*)	5–10 feet	2 x summer/fall
Hornbeam (*Carpinus betulus*)	5–20 feet	1 x late summer

informal hedges

Evergreen hedges	Ideal maximum height	Best times for clipping
Barberry (*Berberis darwinii*)	5–8 feet	1 x after flowering
Cotoneaster (*Cotoneaster lacteus*)	5–7 feet	1 x after fruiting
Firethorn (*Pyracantha*)	6½–10 feet	2 x after flowering and in fall, but avoid berries
Holly (*Ilex aquifolium*)	6½–13 feet	1 x late summer
Privet (*Ligustrum*)	6–8 feet	2 x anytime
Tassel bush (*Garrya elliptica*)	5–7 feet	1 x after flowering
Viburnum tinus	3–8 feet	1 x after flowering
Deciduous hedges		
Barberry (*Berberis thunbergii*)	1–4 feet	1 x after flowering
Forsythia × intermedia	5–8 feet	1 x after flowering
Hawthorn (*Crataegus monogyna*)	5–10 feet	1 x winter
Rosa rugosa	3–5 feet	1 x after flowering

hedge clipping

1 When working with new hedges or hedges that need reshaping, place an upright post at each end of the hedge and stretch a string between them set at the desired height. This will give you a guide to the height without your having to step back all the time, but beware of cutting through the line.

3 Once the hedge has reached the height you require, cut the top down by about 12 inches. This encourages the upper shoots to thicken and bush out, and any stumps from the pruning cuts will be hidden by new growth. With formal evergreen hedges, remember to maintain the sloping angle so the bottom is wider than the top.

2 Start at the bottom of a hedge and work upward so that clippings fall out of the way. If a hedge trimmer is used, cut upward with a sweeping, arclike action, keeping the cutting bar parallel to the hedge. For safety with hedges more than 6 feet high, use two step ladders with a standing board between them.

training fruit trees

There are various methods of growing fruit trees, but generally the trees are either free-standing or trained. Trained trees are those that are grown into a formal shape and in a single plane, usually against a wall, fence, or some other means of support. The purposes of wall-training are to produce high-quality fruits in a relatively confined space and to provide shelter as well as additional warmth for plants such as peaches and nectarines that may not be fully hardy. Two of the most commonly encountered forms of trained fruit trees are the espalier and the fan.

MATERIALS & EQUIPMENT

pruners

garden twine

wire

stakes

lawn care

Lawn care is a year-round task. In spring, as the grass starts to grow, mowing becomes a regular task. To sustain this growth, the lawn needs to be fed and any weeds killed. There is also usually some repair work to do, such as redefining edges or filling any hollows that have formed over the winter. The summer season is when the lawn should be at its best and you can enjoy it to its full. However, there are still maintenance tasks requiring attention. In the fall, mowing is reduced, but other jobs, such as scarifying and treating moss, become important. Diseases are also prevalent in the fall; fungi and insect pests thrive when the soil is warm and the air moist, and this is the time to act to encourage a healthy lawn for the following year.

the essentials

There are a number of tools you will need to keep your lawn in optimum condition. The size and type of lawn you have will dictate some of your choices. However, everyone needs a lawn mower, because regular mowing to the correct height prevents the grass from becoming yellow and uneven and also prevents scalping.

cutting equipment

For mowing the lawn, both reel and rotary mowers are capable of creating a striped effect if fitted with a roller behind the cutting blades; and the hover is useful for creating an even cut on awkward-shaped lawns. Other manual tools are used for neatening the edges, either by cutting through the sod or clipping the grass.

Reel mowers
Reel mowers have a number of spirally arranged cutting blades positioned to form a cylinder. The blades can be manual or powered and cut against a fixed blade in a scissors action.

Rotary mowers
These have one or more blades, or a toughened nylon cord that rotates horizontally at very high speed, slicing through the grass. They work particularly well on long or tough grass.

Hover mowers
Hover mowers are similar to rotary-type mowers, except that they ride on a cushion of air. They are light and easy to use and particularly good for small lawns and awkward-shaped lawns.

Edging shears
These shears, with handles set at right angles to the cutting blades, are used in a standing position for trimming the grass growing over the lawn edge.

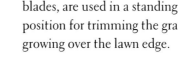

Half-moon edger
This special tool is used for cutting sod and trimming lawn edges. The curved blade is mounted onto a spade shaft and handle for easy use.

general equipment

A garden fork is ideal for easing, lifting, and spiking the lawn, using the tines to alleviate soil compaction. To rake out moss, collect leaves, and remove debris from the lawn, use a fan rake, and for scattering dew, spreading topdressing, and breaking up worm casts, use a stiff brush. A fertilizer spreader is another useful piece of equipment for applying powdered fertilizer evenly.

watering equipment

Static sprinkler
A spinning head distributes water in a circular pattern; the area covered depends on the water pressure.

Rotary sprinkler
The rotating arms provide an even distribution over a wide area (depending on water pressure). Some have adjustable nozzles to regulate the size of the water droplets.

Oscillating sprinkler
A tube with nozzles mounted in a line provides a fan-shaped water pattern. The arm is driven from side-to-side in an arc, spraying water. The speed of rotation is governed by water pressure.

Pulse-jet sprinkler
A nozzle rotates in a series of pulses, distributing an arc of water to cover all or parts of a circular pattern.

Lay-flat sprinkler hose
A flattened garden hose punctured with a series of holes provides a fine spray over the grass at high pressure, or at low pressure the water weeps gently from the hose. This system works particularly well in areas of low water pressure.

first spring cutting

1   As soon as the grass shows signs of new growth, use a fan rake to rake away all traces of dead grass, debris, and worm casts that have accumulated on the lawn during the winter.

2   The grass may be quite long at the beginning of spring, so trying to cut the lawn too short may result in clogging the mower, damaging the machine, and scalping the grass, the latter of which may encourage moss and weeds to grow in the lawn. To avoid this, set the blades on the highest possible setting to encourage growth from the base and root development.

3   Choose a dry day to mow your lawn, as wet grass can produce an untidy effect once it has dried out. Check that there are no stones or branches on the lawn and start mowing by moving forward at a steady pace.

4   Take away the grass clippings. Clean and store the mower, and lower the mower blades, ready for the next cut that will be needed in about a week.

5   The lawn edge can be cut at the beginning of the season with a half-moon edger to redefine the perimeter of the lawn. Place a plank on the edge of the lawn as a guide and to protect the grass. After this, keep the edge trimmed with edging shears (see page 156).

157

mowing

To maintain a healthy lawn, mowing must be carried out regularly throughout the summer. The best approach is to mow little and often, although the frequency of mowing will depend on a number of factors, such as the amount of summer rainfall, the different grasses that make up the lawn and how vigorous they are, and the type of lawn desired—whether it is an ornamental backdrop or a hard-wearing play area.

cutting actions

Reel mower
A scissorlike cutting action traps the grass between moving blades and a lower stationary blade. The number of blades and the speed of rotation determine the fineness of the cut.

Rotary mower
The grass is cut by a high-speed, horizontally rotating blade, and the cutting height is adjusted by raising or lowering wheels or rollers. This type is useful for cutting longer grass.

Hover mower
This type has a scythelike cutting action identical to that of a rotary mower, but the hover mower is actually held over the grass on a cushion of air, which makes it lighter to use.

timing

The mowing season usually lasts from mid-spring through the middle of fall, peaking in the early summer, when the grass is growing at its fastest annual rate. After this period, growth will slow down, as the grass species and cultivars try to produce flower heads and seed. Drier weather conditions also discourage rapid extension growth.

weather

The type of mowing used depends on the prevailing weather conditions. When the weather has been dry for a long period or if it is hot and sunny, mow at a slightly higher setting to leave the grass blades longer to shade their roots. This reduces the stress caused by drought and lessens the amount of watering required. After heavy rainfall, mow frequently, but at a high setting. Cutting the grass very short, or "scalping," weakens the shoots and encourages the establishment of moss and weeds. If the lawn is very wet, a hover-type mower can be run over the grass, either at a very high setting or with the blades removed. This will blow the water from the grass and make it dry enough to mow properly within half an hour.

height

Resist the temptation to cut the grass very short in the hope that it will be a long time before it needs cutting again, as this allows moss and weeds to establish themselves while the grass struggles to recuperate. The golden rule is never to reduce the height of the grass by more than one-third at a single cut, and always allow the grass to recover for a couple of days before cutting it again.

Mowing heights and frequencies		
Lawn type	Height	Mowings per week
Very fine ornamental	½ inch	2–3
Average garden	1 inch	1–2
Hard-wearing (play area)	1½ inches	1

collecting the clippings

Always remove the clippings from the lawn after mowing. Any left behind seldom decompose fully, and they form a layer of dead grass, or "thatch," over the soil. This layer can cause yellow patches, prevents water and fertilizer from reaching the roots, harbors pests and diseases, and encourages cast-forming worms. If your mower does not have a bag to pick up clippings, remove them with a spring-tine rake. Add them to the compost pile unless the grass has just been treated with chemicals. Remember that removing the clippings means that more fertilizer has to be used to keep the lawn healthy.

edge trimming

The edges of the lawn need to be trimmed regularly to prevent them from becoming ragged and untidy. At the start of the season, cut a clean edge to the lawn with a half-moon edging tool; the best time to do this is after the very first mowing of the season.

1   When cutting a new edge to the lawn, it is easier to achieve a straight line if you use a wooden plank as a guide. Lay the plank on the lawn, close to the edge, and cut against it, clearing the soil and grass away as you work. This should be done only once a year, or the lawn will gradually become smaller.

2   After every mowing, the edge can be trimmed with long-handled shears to remove any grass hanging over on the flowerbeds or paths. For the best effect, cut the grass back as close to the edge as you can. Always remove the grass trimmings and collect them along with the clippings from the mower.

common pests

Spotting pests quickly is the surest way to prevent them from doing lasting damage to your lawn. Once they become apparent, there are several ways to eradicate them—from chemical methods to removing the offenders by hand.

Earthworms

Symptoms Unsightly coils of sticky brown soil deposits (casts) appear on the lawn.

Control Worm deterrents: Lower the pH of the soil with acidic fertilizers. Wormkillers: apply a drench of wormkiller in the fall as a last resort.

White grubs

Symptoms White flat grubs with a black-brown head, usually curled up into a C shape. Small brown patches of grass appear in spring and summer as the grubs feed on grass roots.

Control Feed and water the lawn. Apply insecticide or beneficial nematodes.

Leatherjackets

Symptoms These gray-brown legless grubs are found on poorly drained lawns after a wet fall. In the spring they cause yellow patches from feeding on the roots of the grass.

Control Aerate the lawn, and if necessary apply an appropriate insecticide.

Moles

Symptoms Large heaps of soil appear on the surface of the lawn, with holes in the lawn as the burrows collapse.

Control Reduce the mole's food supply by discouraging grubs and worms. Alternatively, call in a mole catcher.

worm management

Most worms prefer a soil temperature of about 50°F and will burrow deeper into the soil to maintain this when surface temperatures are colder. Evidence of worm activity tends to be more obvious in the spring and fall, when they are at their most active; they are rarely seen in the summer, when they are resting deeper in the soil.

Beneficial activity of worms

Worms are essential for good soil conditions, as they drag dead plant material such as grass clippings and thatch underground and mix it with soil, recycling the nutrients that are present in the decaying matter. They also help the movement of air into the soil as they tunnel and improve drainage.

Controlling worms

If you really feel that the only way to have a good ornamental lawn is to reduce the worms in the soil, you can discourage high worm populations by collecting the grass clippings after mowing or by following one of the solutions outlined here.

Wormkillers

Some chemicals can be applied that will only kill the worms that form casts on the soil surface but will not harm other species of worm. Conveniently, those worms that are killed die in situ and are never seen again. However, it must be stressed that using wormkillers should be considered a last resort, since worms are more beneficial than not.

Worm deterrents

Worms prefer a soil pH of between 5.5 and 8.5 and dislike acid soils, so lowering the pH of the soil with acidic fertilizers, such as sulfate of ammonia, will encourage the worms to move out of the

lawn and into the surrounding beds. Use a special kit to check pH levels; acid soils are indicated by yellow or orange, neutral is a pale green, and alkaline is dark green.

watering

In an average year, a well-kept lawn should be able to survive without watering for at least two-thirds of the year. However, in the height of the summer or in long dry periods, the lawn may become stressed due to a lack of water, and irrigation may be needed. The challenge is to spot the first signs of stress and deal with the problem before it becomes acute.

when to water

A lawn needs to be watered as soon as the first signs of drought start to appear. The symptoms to look for are dull, bluish grass with a hard and fibrous texture and footprints remaining for longer than usual because the grass is limp. If the dry weather persists, the leaves of the grass will gradually shrivel and turn brown, and the exposed roots are then in danger of dying off.

how much water to apply

The most common fault is to apply too little water to the lawn, which just encourages the grass to form roots close to the soil surface. These will be the first to dry out in hot weather, making the lawn even more susceptible to drought. Lawns grown on clay soils take much longer to show signs of drought than those grown on light, sandy soils, since clay holds far more water than sand. At the height of summer, in hot, dry weather, a lawn can lose about two inches of water over a week. To replace that would take about 10 gallons of water for every square yard of lawn.

methods of watering

When watering a lawn, the aim is to replace the water that has been lost in the root zone, rather than on the surface. Wet the soil to a depth of at least 6 inches; when it dries out, water again to a depth of 4 inches. On very dry soils it is difficult for the water to penetrate, and it may  form puddles and evaporate, or simply run off on a sloping site. Check the penetration of the water by digging a test hole before and after watering.

To improve drainage on compacted ground, jab the tines of a garden fork into the soil. Work to a depth of 2 inches to make sure the hard crust has been thoroughly penetrated.

The most effective method of watering is to use a low-level sprinkler or soaker hose, both of which apply the water slowly and steadily.

feeding

Frequent mowing removes organic matter from the lawn and, when the clippings are taken away, deprives the grass roots of nutrients; this loss has to be replaced, or the lawn will deteriorate. During the summer, lawns are sometimes seen turning pale green or yellow, a sign of nutrient deficiency. This situation can easily be rectified with a fast-acting nitrogen fertilizer, which will provide the lawn with the boost it needs.

types of fertilizer

To keep the lawn looking green and lush, apply a fast-acting fertilizer, such as sulfate of ammonia, which is high in nitrogen, causing the grass to change color in 7 to 10 days. This comes in liquid, crystal, or dry form. Do not apply too much; you may scorch the grass, which will then turn brown and die.

If the fertilizer is to be applied dry, mix it with soil or sand to avoid scorching the grass. Distribute by hand or fill a special applicator.

applying fertilizer

1   Measure the area of lawn to be fertilized so you can calculate how much fertilizer is needed. Always follow guidelines given by the manufacturer on rates of application.

2   For a liquid fertilizer, measure the correct amount of chemical concentrate or crystals, and pour it into a watering can with a dribble bar. Add warm water, as recommended on the carton.

3   Work over the lawn systematically to cover the whole area with fertilizer, and walk at a steady pace to maintain even distribution.

4   If there is no significant rainfall within two days after an application, water the lawn thoroughly for at least two hours to prevent the fertilizer from scorching the grass.

general maintenance

A lawn is often the largest single feature in a garden, as well as being the most used, but constant wear and tear can result in even the best-kept lawns looking jaded. As use of the lawn tends to decline in the fall, this is the ideal time to follow a regular and well-planned maintenance program, to make sure your lawn is in peak condition for enjoyment throughout the following summer.

soil drainage

Good drainage is essential for maintaining a high-quality lawn. Waterlogging often occurs, however, when the water entering the soil exceeds the amount draining out, and soils that are compacted or have a high percentage of clay in them are particularly vulnerable. The roots of most plants are unable to function properly in waterlogged soil and will eventually die due to lack of oxygen. Wet soils tend to be colder than well-drained ones; this may slow down plant growth in the spring.

Sink

If you have no natural outlet for water, a catchment pit or sink must be constructed so that the water has somewhere to go. This is a rubble-filled pit that holds the excess water from the surrounding drainage  system and is constructed in the lowest part of the garden. Usually the pit is about 5 feet square and 5 feet deep, and is filled with rubble and gravel; the coarse rubble sits in the bottom of the pit, with the finer gravel just below the soil surface. This is particularly effective on compacted soil.

Pipe drains

For a simple single-pipe system, lay the pipes in narrow trenches about 6 inches wide and 2 feet below the surface, on a sloping site. If the site is level, create a slope to encourage the water to drain away quickly. This can be done by laying the pipes 1½ feet deep at the start of the drain, sloping down to 2 feet at the outlet. The pipes are

laid on a bed of gravel and covered with more gravel, then the trench is filled with a 6-inch layer of topsoil.

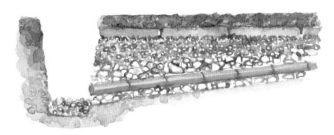

The "herringbone" pattern is the most common drainage system and consists of a main drain, usually 4 inches in diameter and running along the center, with 3-inch-diameter lateral drains running at an angle of 60° into the main drain.

Rubble drains

In small gardens a simple rubble drain will be sufficient for drainage. Narrow trenches 8 to 12 inches wide and 1½ feet deep are used to intercept the water as it passes through the soil, carrying it away from the site. Each trench has a 1-foot layer of coarse rubble, followed by 2 inches of gravel and 4 inches of topsoil.

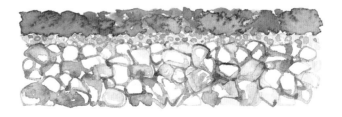

making an ornamental grass garden

If you do not have the time or the climate to grow the fine grasses suitable for a lawn, it is still relatively easy to create an ornamental grass border by using grasses, sedges, and bamboos. In addition to being tough and resilient, grasses vary widely in shape, habit, form, and color, with architectural qualities making them a striking feature in any garden.

MATERIALS & EQUIPMENT

organic matter

garden fork and spade

granular all-purpose fertilizer

container-grown grasses (see page 170)

hand trowel

watering can

mulch (organic or inorganic)

creating a new lawn

Fall and summer are the best times to create a new lawn, particularly while the weather is still mild, by preparing the soil and either sowing seed or laying sod. This will establish a sturdy root system slowly over the winter period that will rapidly grow in the spring. Always begin by removing all traces of weed and incorporating plenty of organic matter to improve moisture retention and soil texture.

creating a new lawn from seed

Lawn grasses are usually divided into two categories: cool-season and warm-season. By mixing different types of seed, you can create a lawn that fits the situation: shady, sunny, or high-traffic. Warm-season grasses—such as zoysia, St. Augustine, and Bermuda—tolerate the heat of the South and are usually grown as single species, started with plugs or sod.

Preparing and sowing the site

1   Rake the soil surface with a fine rake, so that when the seed is sown it will come into contact with moist soil.

2   Using pegs and string, divide the lawn area into 3-foot-square sections and measure 1½ ounces of seed into a container for each square.

3   Sow the seed evenly over each square: sow half of the seed across the area, and then the remainder at a right angle to the first sowing.

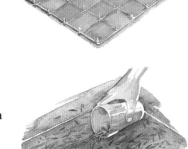

Germination

Sowing seed when the soil is warm and dry on the surface but moist underneath aids rapid germination. In good conditions grass seeds germinate in 10 to 14 days. About three weeks after germination, lightly roll the grass to encourage "tillering" (new clusters of leaves formed from the base) to thicken coverage.

Some suitable cool-season lawn seed mixtures

Hard-wearing lawns
10%	Kentucky tall fescue
40%	Chewings fescue
20%	Creeping red fescue
30%	Perennial ryegrass

Banks and slopes
20%	Colonial bent grass
30%	Chewings fescue
45%	Creeping red fescue
5%	Tall fescue

Fine lawns
20%	Kentucky bluegrass
40%	Chewings fescue
40%	Creeping red fescue

Quick-growing utility lawns
40%	Chewings fescue
30%	Perennial ryegrass
20%	Crested dog's-tail
10%	Rough-stalked meadow grass

Ornamental lawns
20%	Browntop bent
80%	Chewings fescue

Lightly shaded lawns
10%	Colonial bent grass
30%	Chewings fescue
35%	Creeping red fescue
25%	Rough-stalked bluegrass

creating a new lawn from sod

For an instant lawn, sod or turf is used, though this is more expensive than sowing from seed. Sod is best laid in the early fall, when the top growth is slow and the warm, moist soil encourages rapid root growth. Sod is usually cut in 1 x 3-foot sections, rolled along their length for easy transportation and storage. Plan laying your new lawn so you do not store the rolls for more than a few days, because the grass will turn yellow.

1   On a well-prepared site, mark the outside edges of your lawn. Lay out the sods on at least two edges of the area by opening each one out and pressing it firmly into position against the preceding one.

2   Place a plank on the row of sod that has just been laid, to firm the sod into position and prevent it from being damaged. Arrange the sods so the seams are staggered like the pattern of bricks on a house wall.

3   When you need to cut a sod to make it fit, lay one piece over the other one, then trim the lower one to size with a knife so the top piece fits neatly into place.

4   To establish the edges, use a wooden plank or a length of garden twine as a guide for straight edges, and a garden hose or thick rope for curved ones. The best tool to use for cutting the sod is a half-moon edging tool, or a sharp spade.

5   Finally, sweep the surface with a stiff brush to lift the flattened grass and remove any loose stones and soil. If the area is dry, water with a sprinkler.

Mowing
Cut the grass about 10 to 14 days after the sod has been laid, cutting at a height of 1½ inches to check the top growth and encourage root penetration into the soil.

planting ground cover

There are a number of perfectly good alternatives to grass for ground cover that look equally
attractive and also save on mowing. In shady areas, especially beneath trees, grasses often
struggle to survive, but plants such as epimediums, some geraniums, ivies, and *Pachysandra*
will readily cover the soil. Grass on sloping sites and awkward-shaped areas is notoriously
difficult to manage, but plants like baby's tears (*Soleirolia soleirolii*), shown here,
Polygonum affine, *Rubus tricolor*, and thyme all spread and surface-root as they grow,
and can be used to cover and stabilize the soil.

MATERIALS & EQUIPMENT

garden fork

weedkiller

suitable plants (see page 177)

sheets of black plastic or landscape fabric to cover the site

spade

knife

trowel

organic or inorganic mulch

lawn repairs

If a lawn is used regularly, a certain amount of wear and tear is inevitable; edges become ragged or trodden by walking too close to the lawn edge, and bare patches occur due to mower settings being too low or the removal of a mat-forming weed. Although these blemishes look unsightly, they are quite easy to repair and the lawn can recover its health and appearance remarkably quickly.

repairing a damaged lawn edge

1   Mark a square around the damaged area with pegs and string and, using the string as a guide, cut out a square of sod from behind the damaged edge using a half-moon edger.

2   Using a spade or edger, cut horizontally under the sod to a depth of about 2 inches; this will sever the roots so the sod can be lifted up.

3   Lift the section of sod with a spade and turn it 180°, which will place the damaged edge within the lawn and leave a crisp firm outside edge. Gently firm the section of sod back into place until it is level with the surrounding lawn.

4   The original damaged edge is filled with a sandy topdressing or garden soil, and firmed until it is the same level as the lawn. Grass seed is then sown onto the topdressing and watered in. If the weather is dry, place a piece of loosely woven burlap over the seeded area to prevent drying out and encourage rapid germination. Within 6 weeks the area should have fully recovered.

repairing a damaged patch

1   Using a fan rake, rake away all traces of old dead grass and debris to leave the patch of soil bare on the lawn.

2   Then use a hand fork to jab into the surface of the soil to a depth of about ¾ inch; this will break up the surface and ease soil compaction.

3   Then using the fan rake again, rake the surface of the soil to a depth of about 1 inch to create a fine tilth for a seedbed, ready to take the new grass seed.

4   Sow the grass seed evenly over the prepared area, at a rate equivalent to 1 ounce per square yard. Immediately after sowing, lightly rake the seed into the soil surface. A useful tip is to lay a piece of loosely woven burlap over the seeded area to prevent drying out, encourage rapid germination, and deter birds from eating the seed.

repairing humps and hollows

1   Using a half-moon edger, cut two lines into the lawn to form a cross, with the center of the cross in the center of the affected area. Make these cuts large enough that they exceed the area to be leveled.

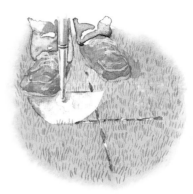

2   Using a spade or edger, cut horizontally under the sod to a depth of about 2 inches. This will sever the roots so the sod can be lifted up. Cutting from the center of the cross out, into, and under the lawn causes less damage to the surface of the lawn.

3   Peel back the four sections of sod to expose the soil beneath; uncover a large area of soil that will allow you plenty of room to work within the affected lawn area.

4   For a hollow, fill the hollow beneath the sod with good-quality topsoil and firm gently until it is level with the surrounding soil. For a hump, remove some soil until it is level with the surrounding soil.

5   Finally, carefully replace the folded sod into its original position and firm gently until it is level with the surrounding lawn, or fractionally higher to allow for settling. Cover this area with a ½-inch layer of sandy

topdressing or sifted garden soil, and then brush it into the seams to encourage them to reestablish their roots quickly.

introducing plants into your lawn

Though frequently undervalued as merely a flat green expanse that often requires a great deal of work, the lawn has an important contribution to make to the garden. A lawn is a basic feature of many gardens and can be purely functional; however, the addition of plants within the lawn area can make it a more colorful and highly ornamental feature.

planting bulbs

Groups of bulbs can be planted beneath the grass in your lawn to introduce interest or lead the eye in a particular direction.

1   Use a half-moon edger or spade to cut an "H" shape in the grass. Cut under the sod with a spade and pull back the edges.

2   Loosen the soil and place the bulbs into the hole in an upright position, and press down into the soil. Then pull the soil back into the hole over the bulbs and firm in.

3   Place the sod back over the bulbs and firm in place. If the soil is dry, water thoroughly immediately after planting to settle the soil around the bulbs and remove any air pockets.

Allium moly

Galanthus 'S. Arnott'

Ornithogalum arabicum

> **Suitable bulbs**
> *Allium moly*
> Snowdrop (*Galanthus*)
> Star-of-Bethlehem
>   (*Ornithogalum*)

planting trees and shrubs

A single tree or shrub adds a focal point in a garden lawn. Be careful, however, in your choice of plant; trees such as birch (*Betula*) and honeylocust (*Gleditsia*) are a good choice since they have a thin canopy and cast only a little shade over the grass.

1 With stakes and string, mark a circle for the hole to at least twice the width of the plant's root system.

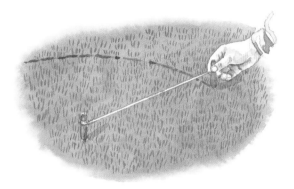

2 Remove the sod with a spade and stack it away from the working area.

3 Dig a hole that is at least twice the width of the plant's root system and deep enough to accommodate all of the roots.

4 Using a garden fork, break up the soil in the bottom of the hole to allow the new roots to spread into the soil surrounding the planting hole.

5 Holding the plant by its stem, carefully place it in the center of the hole, with the root ball on the bottom, and use a bamboo stake to check that the plant is level with the surrounding soil.

6 Start to backfill the hole with soil, spreading it evenly around the roots, and shake the stem of the tree to settle the soil between the roots. This will also remove any air pockets around the roots.

7 Fill the hole with layers of soil and firm each layer with your foot, until the hole has been filled to its original level.

8 Apply a topdressing of fertilizer to the soil around the plant and mix it into the top 2 inches. This will gradually be washed down into the root zone.

making an herb walkway

The use of herbs was very popular in medieval England for carpeting green walkways. Chamomile was widely used, as was thyme, which has the added quality of being covered in a carpet of pinkish-purple flowers in the summer, as well as having a wonderful aroma. Growing a whole lawn can be expensive and time-consuming, since you would need hundreds of plants to create an instant display, so creating walkways around the garden is a much simpler method of introducing small stretches of these attractive plants.

MATERIALS & EQUIPMENT

organic matter such as compost or composted manure

general-purpose fertilizer

trowel, garden fork, and rake

suitable herbs (see page 185)

watering can

Soil preparation

1 Herb lawns will usually occupy the same site for many years, which means that the soil must be well cultivated before planting. Dig over the soil and remove all weeds to reduce weed problems when the lawn is establishing. Incorporate plenty of organic matter to improve moisture retention and texture.

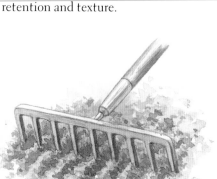

2 Add a dressing of general-purpose fertilizer and mix into the top 4 inches of soil. Then rake the site level.

Planting

3 Choose your herb (here we are illustrating *Chamaemelum nobile* 'Treneague,' but see opposite for other suitable plants), and space the offsets about 6 to 12 inches apart—closer spacing simply means that the lawn will establish quicker. Start by digging a planting hole large enough to accommodate the whole root system. Avoid planting when the soil is wet and sticky, which can lead to compaction that may impede plant establishment.

4 Hold each plant by the stem or leaves and gently remove it from the tray or pot—if the plants come in clumps, you may need to separate them with a knife, but leave as much soil as possible around the roots.

5 Place the plant in the hole with the base of the root ball on the floor of the hole, making sure the top of the hole is level with the top of the root ball.

6 Using a trowel, pull the soil back into the hole around the plant and firm gently into place. Make sure the surface of the root ball is covered by soil.

7 Immediately after planting, water the new lawn to settle the plants and help them establish quickly.

Maintaining the herb lawn

8 Very little mowing is required for many plants, and they need only an occasional trim. Use shears or a rotary mower with the blades set at a height of 2 inches and remove any long or straggly growth.

9 Hand-weeding is the only effective method of control in an herb lawn. There is no acceptable chemical available that will kill the weeds without harming the lawn-making plants, because some weeds, such as yarrow, are very close relatives of the lawn plants.

Other plants suitable for a non-grass lawn

Buttonweed (*Leptinella atrata*)

Chamomile 'Treneague'
  (*Chamaemelum nobile* 'Treneague')

Corsican mint (*Mentha requienii*)

Lawn chamomile
  (*Chamaemelum nobile*)

Pennyroyal (*Mentha pulegium*)

Wild thyme (*Thymus serpyllum*)

pond care

The secret of successful pond care is doing the right thing at the right time. The pond calendar year really begins in spring, as water temperatures rise, fish become more active, and frogs come out of hibernation and begin to breed. Many water plants and marginals are also propagated at this time of year. The summer should be the time to sit back and enjoy the pond, but if left to their own devices, many of the plants will become too large, crowding out their less vigorous neighbors, so plants have to be lifted and divided. It is all too easy to put the pond to the back of your mind once the water lilies have gone over, but preparation in the fall will help to determine how well the pond and its contents survive the winter.

pond maintenance

General pond maintenance tends to be fairly minimal if carried out on a regular basis, and you need not empty the pond every year unless it has been neglected. After a number of years, however, silt and debris will accumulate on the floor of the pond, which may lead to pollution levels so bad that both plants and fish begin to suffer. But the water of even a healthy pond is quite literally alive with masses of microscopic plants and other organisms. In the summer, unfortunately, some of them can multiply so rapidly that they have a detrimental effect on the quality of the water. Weeds are also at their most prolific during the summer season. Both can have an adverse effect on the pond plants as well as the fish, so keep a watchful eye and resolve any problems as soon as they become apparent. Leaks may also occur as a result of frost damage, ground subsidence or heave, or even deterioration through age. Any leaks must be dealt with as soon as you notice them.

water color

Brown, murky water is often the sign of a healthy ecosystem. It usually means fish are actively feeding at the bottom of the pond, or breeding. It may take a few weeks for a new pond to come into balance. However, if the water is blue or black, or has a thick whitish scum floating on the surface and foul-smelling bubbles, the pond has probably become polluted by rotting vegetation on its bottom. This robs the water of oxygen and may kill fish and water snails. The only long-term solution is to clean the pond (see opposite).

1   First remove the fish and plants from the pond and store in buckets of water. Drain the pond using a pump, or siphon off the water.

2   The debris that has collected in the bottom can then be scooped out and the lining cleaned. Refill the pond, but before returning the plants and the fish, let the water settle and warm up slightly.

pond water pH

Ideally the pond water should be slightly acid to alkaline, that is between 6.5 and 8.5 on the pH scale. If your water gives a higher or lower reading than this, the plants and fish may suffer. Check the pH level regularly with a special kit available from pet stores or some garden centers. You can use hydrated lime to raise the pH, but add only a small amount at a time to allow the pond life to adapt to the new conditions.

water levels

In hot, dry weather, the water level in the pond can drop by as much as 2 inches over a week due to evaporation. Topping up the water regularly will help to prevent the liner from cracking in the heat, especially if it is plastic. The addition of fresh water will also help to keep the fish and plants healthy. When topping up, let the water cascade into the pond from a height of about 3 feet. This creates the turbulence that is necessary to introduce more oxygen into the water.

pond cleaning

When a thorough clean is required, choose a mild day in late spring, when the water is clear and it is easy to see the plants and fish in the pond. Temporary storage for the plants and fish can include barrels, buckets, or even large plastic bags.

1 Store any fish that are taken from the pond in containers, and keep them in water consisting of half clean water and half pond water, to help prevent the fish from suffering from shock or stress.

2 Remove as many of the plants as possible before lowering the water level, taking out the marginal plants first, the deep-water aquatics when some of the water has been drained away, and the floaters and oxygenators when they are within reach.

3 Completely drain the pond of water. To do this, use an electric pump, bail out, or siphon off the water.

4 Then remove all silt and debris from the bottom of the pond and scrub the walls with a stiff-bristled brush, regularly dipping it in clean water, but take care not to damage the lining of the pond.

5 After the pond has been cleaned, leave the sides to dry for a few hours, to kill off any pest and disease residue that may have escaped the cleaning process. Refill the pond with slow-running water.

6 Add the plants to be submerged by lowering them gently into the water when it is almost up to the required level, adding the marginals and floating plants last, once the water is starting to clear. Do not introduce the fish until the water is almost clear, as they may suffocate due to the particles in the cloudy water clogging their gills.

spotting and repairing a leak

If the water level in your pond falls, do not automatically assume that it has a leak; it may be due to surface evaporation, especially in hot or windy weather. A constant drop in water level during cool, still weather is usually the first indication of a leak, and one of the most common causes of damage to the pond liner is frost damage, which usually shows up in the spring. Let the water level fall and stabilize, since this will indicate the level of the damaged area. The first stage is to empty the pond: follow steps 1 to 3 as for "Pond Cleaning" (see page 189), then brush away any dirt or weed residue and let it dry.

Repairing flexible liners

1   Cut a patch from a liner repair sheet at least twice as long and twice as wide as the damaged area, and clean the patch and the damaged area with denatured alcohol (to give good adhesion).

2   Apply a liberal covering of waterproof bonding cement or double-sided adhesive to both the patch and the damaged area of the liner.

3   When the adhesive feels "tacky," place the patch over the damaged area and smooth it down to make a good bonding and remove any air bubbles. Check the repair after 24 hours, and if it is firmly bonded to the liner, refill the pond (steps 5 and 6 in "Pond Cleaning," page 189).

Concrete liner

1   Using a hammer and mason's chisel, chisel out some of the concrete around the crack to make it a little wider than the original damaged section—this will help to strengthen the final repair.

2   Brush out all loose dirt and debris from the crack and carefully fill the crack with a special waterproof mastic cement.

3   Once the mastic cement is dry, paint the whole lining of the pond with two to three coatings of waterproof pond sealant. Leave it to dry for at least 24 hours, and then refill the pond (see steps 5 and 6 in "Pond Cleaning," page 189).

making a small pond

In many respects, the basic question about making a pond is a simple one—
how to make a hole in the ground that will hold water for long periods of time.
The solution is to line the hole with some form of waterproof material, and
there is a wealth of choice, including concrete, flexible and semirigid liners,
and molded preformed liners. Flexible liners are often the best solution
because they can be molded into any shape. They are economical, light for
handling, and they are not damaged as easily in cold-winter areas.

MATERIALS & EQUIPMENT

length of hose or rope

spade

plank and level

old carpet or fiberglass insulation material to fit hole

synthetic rubber or plastic lining sheet to fit hole

slabs or bricks for edge

mortar

pond plants (see page 194)

introducing new plants

Aquatic plants should be moved or transplanted while they are actively growing, as they reestablish better if moved during the growing season. The best time to move them is in the late spring, which will give them the maximum period of time to establish themselves in their new surroundings before the onset of winter.

planting aquatics

Most aquatics are planted and grown in submerged basketlike containers, the advantages being that it gives the gardener a greater degree of control over the plants' growing environment and makes them more accessible for inspection and propagation. The usual material used for containers is heavy-gauge rigid plastic. Wood and metal containers should be avoided because they produce toxins harmful to fish.

If you are planting water lilies, trim any rotting or dead sections of rootstock and any damaged leaves before planting.

1   Line the mesh container with sacking or heavy-gauge paper, to stop the soil from spilling out through the mesh.

2   Half-fill the basket with medium and trim off any surplus liner around the outside of the container.

3   Place the plant firmly in the center of the basket, add more medium, and pack it around the plant so it is held firmly in position.

4   Fill the basket until the medium is 1 inch from the rim and top with a ½-inch layer of gravel over the soil.

5   Water the container thoroughly to soak the plant and help settle the soil around the roots.

6   To lower the basket into the pond, it is a good idea to attach string handles to the sides of the basket, so you do not have to drop it into place.

summer planting

Aquatic plants of all types are best planted in the late spring and early summer, but planting can be delayed until the late summer. Those that are planted later will simply have less time to become established before the winter, although some may not fully recover until the following spring. Choose different types of plants—floaters, oxygenators, and deep-water aquatics—to create a balanced environment within the pond, and fertilize them as they develop to maintain their health.

pond and bog plants

For a water feature of any size to be effective and provide the ideal environment for fish and other pond life to live and breed successfully, plants must be present. They provide food, shade, and shelter, as well as help keep the water sweet and clear.

Deep-water aquatics
Growing up from a depth of about 2 feet, these provide shelter for fish and help to keep the water clear.

Bog plants
These are ideal for a marshy area surrounding the pond as they prefer a rich, peaty, damp soil that will keep their roots cool. Most bog plants are herbaceous perennials and benefit from being lifted and divided every three years or so.

Floaters
Plants in this group have their leaves and stems on the pond surface, with their roots submerged. They reduce the amount of light reaching the water, so they help to exclude algae.

Marginals
This diverse group of plants thrives in shallow water or damp soil, depending on the species. Marginals are largely decorative, although they do attract insects and provide cover for other wildlife.

Oxygenators
These plants help to keep the water aerated, as they release oxygen as a by-product of photosynthesis. Oxygenators should be fully submerged, with only the flowers on or above the surface. Aim to include about three oxygenating plants per square yard of pond surface.

Deep-water aquatics
Aponogeton distachyos
Nymphaea
Nymphoides peltata

Bog plants
Lobelia × gerardii
Matteuccia struthiopteris

Floaters
Hydrocharis morsus-ranae
Lemna trisulca
Stratiotes aloides

Marginals
Calla palustris
Juncus effusus 'Spiralis'

Oxygenators
Chara aspera
Elodea canadensis
Myriophyllum spicatum

propagation

Many water plants will be flowering and growing rapidly in this season, often providing suitable material with which to increase your stocks, whether from seeds or cuttings. Some may even have exceeded their allotted area and will need lifting and dividing into smaller plants to maintain a balanced population and prevent overcrowding. For many of these tasks, the earlier in the summer they are carried out, the more rapidly the individual plants and the pond as a whole will recover.

seed-raised plants

Many of the bog plants and marginals around the edge of the pond can be increased by raising new plants from their seed, collected after flowering. In most cases, these seeds can be sown fresh, immediately after collection, but they may need some protection over the winter; seeds of pickerel weed (*Pontederia*), for instance, will not germinate until the following spring.

Seed sowing

1   Select a seed tray (modular trays are best if seedlings are to stay in the tray a long time) and fill with soil. Firm gently to within ½ inch of the rim. For very fine seeds, sift a thin layer of soil over the surface.

2   Sow the seed as evenly as possible over the surface. Place larger seeds individually on the soil and press in lightly.

3   Sift a thin layer of fine soil over the seeds and firm the soil gently. Press very fine seeds gently onto the surface rather than trying to cover them with more soil, or they may become too deeply buried.

4   Remember to write the name of the plant and the date the seeds were sown on a label and insert it at the end of the tray.

5   Place the seed tray in a shallow container of water so the soil takes up water by capillary action, then allow the surplus water to drain away. This method does not disturb the seeds, making it much safer than overhead watering.

6   Cover the seed tray with a piece of clear glass and a sheet of newspaper to provide the seeds with shade and to prevent the soil from drying out. Place the completed tray in a propagating case or a cold frame to provide a warm, humid environment that will encourage the seeds to germinate.

making a pebble pond

A pebble pond with a fountain of water jetting through the center makes an unusual
and attractive feature in any garden, and can be adapted in size to suit the space
available. A metal or plastic tank, or even a tub, is simply inserted into the ground
to act as a reservoir and to house the submersible pump; the decorative pebbles
are then suspended above it on a metal grate. Add shells to the collection of pebbles
if you have any; the water splashing over them will highlight the shiny surfaces,
as well as bring out any interesting colors or markings.

MATERIALS & EQUIPMENT

peg and string

garden spade

coarse gravel and sand

24 x 18 x 22-inch tank or tub made from plastic or galvanized steel

flexible pond liner

submersible pump

waterproof tape

rigid pipe

metal grate

pebbles

controlling weeds

As light levels increase in the spring, not only do the ornamental plants begin to grow, but so do the weeds. New ponds where the natural water balance is not yet fully established are particularly susceptible, but it is worth waiting for the pond to settle before taking any drastic action to remove the weeds. The introduction of healthy plants, including oxygenators, helps to starve weeds of necessary light and nutrients, and should stop their growth; however, you will almost certainly encounter some that appear to be increasing and will need to be eradicated.

Blanket weed

This is a type of algae that uses light and the nitrogen in the water to grow rapidly in mid-spring. Thick layers of blanket weed can be effectively cleared by dragging it out on a stick or a garden rake. The weed may contain beneficial insects and water snails, so to avoid removing too many of these, leave the piles of blanket weed on the side of the pond overnight to give any creatures the chance to crawl back into the water. For more persistent cases of blanket weed, chemical controls are available.

Duckweed

Duckweed is mainly found growing on still water. This weed is made up of small clusters of leaves with roots attached to them that hang into the water. It does have some beneficial effect—the fish really seem to enjoy eating it—but it quickly covers the surface of the pond, blocking out the light and killing or considerably weakening submerged plants. Drag it out with a fine-gauge net or colander, and always make sure at least one-third of the water's surface area is kept free of duckweed.

An effective preventive measure is to float a burlap sack of straw or hay in the pond in early spring. Another useful and easy trick is to stuff the hay into an old pair of panty hose, secured at the end with a knot, that can then be thrown into the pond. Nitrogen used by bacteria to attack the hay then deprives the blanket weed of the necessary nutrients to develop any further.

fish care

If you already have fish established in your pond, you will notice that they become more active in spring, as their rate of metabolism increases. As they start to move around, they will need to be fed liberally to build up their strength that will also help them to fight disease, which is particularly prevalent in this season. For new ponds, now is the time to introduce your fish to their new home, once the severe weather has passed.

looking after your fish

In an established pond, regular feeding of the fish in spring and summer may not always be necessary, due to the insect population living in and around the pond. Make sure you do not overfeed the fish in the pond since this can be harmful, especially in a small pond where uneaten food decomposes and pollutes the water.

Watch the movement of the fish to monitor any change in their behavior. The usual signs of potential problems are either slow and sluggish behavior from individual fish, while others remain active, or frenzied swimming, frequent surfacing, and body rubbing against the side of the pond. If a problem is suspected, it is a good idea to have a closer look at them; lift them with a net and place them in a separate container for examination so that the correct treatment can then be administered.

introducing new fish

An average initial stocking rate is ten fish to every 3 square feet of pond surface. Hardy fish that can live together include the common goldfish, the longer-tailed comet goldfish, rudd, and golden orfe (which are particularly useful as they eat mosquito larvae). Golden orfe and rudd should be introduced in quantity since they naturally prefer to swim in schools.

New fish are usually transported in plastic bags part-filled with water and inflated with oxygen. Ideally, the pond should have been planted at least a month before the fish are introduced to allow the plants to develop new roots and establish sufficiently to start producing new growth. It takes this amount of time to establish an ecological balance within the pond.

1   Place the container holding the fish on the surface of the pond to allow the water in the pond and the container to reach the same temperature. This will prevent the fish from suffering temperature shock when they are released.

2   After 2 to 3 hours you can open the container and tip the fish into their new environment. Tilt it into the pond water, allowing the fish to adjust and swim slowly into the pond. After an hour, scatter some food over the surface of the pond.

routine care

The growing seasons are exciting times with the introduction of new plants and features, and they are also a period of rapid growth for new and established plants. However, in order to maintain a healthy and attractive garden, there are routine tasks that must be attended to. The beginning of the spring season is ideal for attending to the maintenance of garden buildings and structures and for checking that tools and machinery are in good working order. In summer, do not be seduced into thinking that the garden can look after itself. A summer that brings more or less rain than usual will be one that requires action on your part, but no matter what the weather, pruning, feeding, deadheading, and training are on-going tasks.

forms of winter protection

A combination of frozen soil and cold, drying winds can cause rapid moisture loss that cannot be replaced by a plant's root system. This situation results in the death of leaves and soft shoot tips. Although some plants are tough enough to withstand cold winter temperatures, many need an extra covering to shield them from unfavorable conditions. There are several different materials and methods available for sheltering the plants in your garden. Natural protection comes in the form of hedges, such as yew (*Taxus*), which provide a dense barrier of defense, or from sturdy woven fences. Alternatively, you can construct your own forms of protection using any of the materials below.

burlap

Protecting plants will effectively screen them from extreme weather conditions. A burlap tepee constructed in mid-fall will prevent wind damage to the branches and stems, as well as protecting from frost and preventing any further water loss. A tepee shape is the most effective design, since it shields the top growth and still permits air to circulate, allowing the plants to breathe. If the weather gets warmer, one side can be opened and tied back, or in even milder conditions, the protection can simply be removed. If the support structure is left in place during the winter period, the plant can be protected quickly and easily if the weather becomes suddenly cold and windy again.

1   For the example shown here, we have chosen to protect a *Viburnum tinus*. Start by selecting four sturdy 5-foot stakes (alter the size to fit your plant) and push them into the soil in an upight position. Each stake should be 1 foot away from the plant, forming a square.

2   Draw the tops of each of the four stakes in so they come together directly over the plant. Tie the stakes together with string. This forms the basic framework of the tepee, which can be left in place throughout the winter and used to support the burlap cover when needed.

3   For the outer protective layer, use burlap, plastic mesh, or even thick newspaper. Measure the area to be covered and cut out your material, then wrap it around three sides of the tepee and attach it to the stakes with twist ties. Leave the sheltered side open, but seal it off in bad weather.

4   As an extra protective measure, if temperatures drop very low, fill the cavity between the plant and the wrapping with straw, packing it lightly around the leaves and branches. Alternatively, wrap extra layers of covering material around the outside of the protective frame, securing as before.

214

cloches

These are best used for small numbers of low-growing plants that need protecting during winter, such as annuals sown in fall, alpines, or overwintering vegetables. The simplest form of cloche can be made from plastic stretched over, and held in place by, wire hoops. The advantage of this type is that you can close off the end by gathering the sheet together and wrapping it around a wooden peg. A sturdier alternative is corrugated plastic or Plexiglas, which can be bent into an arch and held down with metal pegs. At the top of the line are glass cloches, but these tend to be very expensive. Plastic and Plexiglas offer the most effective frost protection, but they lose heat quickly in the late afternoon and evening, with temperatures being lower under the cloches than outside on occasion.

Plastic sheeting over wire hoops   *A corrugated plastic arch*

polyethylene

This material is readily available and easy to apply. Tie it in place or anchor it down with bricks, making sure it does not touch the plants themselves, and leave a gap for air to get in and out. Plastic lets  the air around the plants get very hot during the day, but gives way to rapid heat loss during the night, so it is better used as a short-term backup.

fleece

Loosely woven or spun materials provide better protection than plastic sheeting, with far less temperature fluctuation. They are good for wrapping around plants such as conifers and broad-leaved evergreens. Use them in either sheets or strips, and secure to your plant with string tied loosely around the outside in three or four places. Fleece can also be spread over the top of low-growing tender plants and vegetables. To hold it in place, make large staples out of thin wire and push them through the fleece and into the soil beneath. This type of insulator does not become very hot during the day, but it retains its heat well and keeps plants warm during the night. In areas where wind chill is particularly bad, do not worry about keeping this covering in place from fall right through to early spring, since light and air can still penetrate it.

windbreaks

The best material to use for windbreaks is webbing or netting and polypropylene with 50 percent permeability. This flexible mesh allows light, air, and rain to filter through to the plant, but reduces the impact of strong winds and frost. You can buy ready-made windbreaks or construct your own. Using one of the recommended materials, attach lengths between posts or stakes at regular intervals, zigzagging between plants for the most effective protection. Good for plants with weak stems, these screens can range in height from about 20 inches up to 12 feet.

patio and container-grown plants

The majority of popular plants grown outdoors in containers are from temperate and subtropical areas, and grow best in a temperature range of 50 to 65°F. These plants are very susceptible to frost damage, particularly around the roots. If you are unable to bring your containers indoors over winter, you can protect them with a suitable insulation material.

wrapping a small container-grown plant

1　Lay the container on its side, making sure you do not crack or break it. Wrap it with burlap, bubble plastic, old carpet, or cardboard. If you cannot lay your container down, simply wrap the insulation material around the sides.

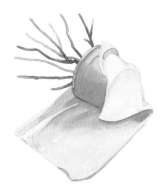

2　In severe cold, straw can be used as an additional insulator. Place wads of straw between the branches of the plant, then gather up the branches and tie them loosely together so the straw is held in position between the branches.

3　For further protection against wet weather, make your covering waterproof by wrapping a layer of plastic film or sheeting around the insulation material already in place. Remove it when the threat of rain or snow has passed.

Root-killing temperatures for container-grown ornamentals

32 to 23°F
Common box
　(*Buxus sempervirens*)
Garland flower
　(*Daphne cneorum*)
Magnolia × *soulangeana*
Mahonia japonica
St. John's wort (*Hypericum*)

23 to 18°F
Flowering dogwood
　(*Cornus florida*)
Japanese cedar
　(*Cryptomeria japonica*)
Japanese maple
　(*Acer palmatum*)
Star magnolia
　(*Magnolia stellata*)

18 to 5°F
Chinese juniper
　(*Juniperus chinensis*)
Oregon grape
　(*Mahonia aquifolium*)
Switch ivy
　(*Leucothoe fontanesiana*)
Viburnum carlesii

Buxus sempervirens

Acer palmatum

Juniperus

packing a large container-grown plant

1   Begin by crushing sheets of wastepaper (single sheets of newspaper are ideal, and provided it is kept dry, it has very good insulating properties) into balls, roughly equal to the size of a tennis ball.

2   Place the prepared balls of paper in plastic garbage bags; the bags should be full but not too tightly packed. Close up the tops and tie them with string.

3   The paper-filled bags are then packed neatly around the sides of the container. Tie the bundles in place with string to make sure they do not blow away.

enclosing large containers

1   A useful method for protecting plants in large, heavy containers is to place 4-inch wads of straw between two layers of chicken wire. Cut the chicken wire so it is slightly taller than the plant and container and wide enough to fully enclose it.

2   Join the four edges of the wire by twisting it together at the corners. Enclose the container and plant with the straw coat and join the outer edges by twisting the end wires.

3   During the coldest weather it is a good idea to construct a lid to fit over the straw and chicken wire coat. Cut chicken wire into two circles, place wads of straw between them, and then twist the wires together around the perimeter. Place the finished straw lid on top of the side covering. It can easily be removed when the weather conditions improve.

217

making a raised bed

A raised planter provides a neat, clearly defined growing area where it is possible to work without having to stoop or bend too much. The height and shape add an extra dimension to the garden and a new growing surface. The soil used can be of a different type to the surrounding soil, allowing, for example, acid-loving plants such as rhododendrons to be grown even when the surrounding soil is alkaline. Plants such as alpines that like a dry or free-draining site also do very well in this slightly elevated growing environment.

MATERIALS & EQUIPMENT

pegs and string

hand fork or garden fork

heavy wooden beams, or logs of uniform size and thickness

galvanized nails, 6 inches long, and hammer

coarse gravel and stones

old carpet or pieces of sod

potting soil to suit chosen plants

plants of your choice to suit the soil

Measuring out the bed

1 Using string and wooden pegs, mark the area
and dimensions of the raised bed.

2 Remove any surface vegetation and weeds from within the
marked area. For small areas, use a hand fork and pull the weeds
by hand; for larger beds, turn the soil with a garden fork.

Making the bed

3 Heavy wooden beams are ideal for creating a raised bed;
however, an equally attractive effect can be created using logs.
The broad dimensions and weight of beams and logs mean that
no concrete or broken brick foundation layer is necessary. Start by
placing the bottom layer where indicated by the string and pegs.
Leave a 1-inch open gap between the end of each beam or log to
provide space for surplus water to drain away freely; cut the wood
where necessary to fit your bed.

4 Repeat the process, working around the wall
to raise the height of the wall around the planting
bed. If you are using beams, it is a good idea to
stagger them like bricks, to make the structure
more stable. Two layers will make a low wall, or
for a bed about knee high, use four layers.

5   Although the weight of the wood means that the structure will be fairly stable as it is, it is a good idea to secure it further with nails. Start by driving 6-inch nails into the corner joints at an angle. Then to anchor the top row in position, drive more 6-inch nails through the vertical joints, again positioning the nails at an angle.

6   Now that the structure is in place, you can prepare the bed for planting. Start by filling the lower quarter of the bed with coarse gravel and stones to form a drainage layer, and cover this layer over with inverted pieces of sod or, if you do not have any, a section of old carpet or landscape fabric will work just as well—this is to prevent any soil being washed into the gravel below, which will restrict the drainage effect.

7   Fill the remaining three-quarters of the bed with soil, potting medium, or a mixture of both. Do not pack this layer, but allow it to settle during planting so it is about 2 to 3 inches below the rim of the bed.

Planting up the bed

8   Choose and plant suitable plants for your bed (see "New Introductions" on pages 12–26 for planting techniques). Raised beds are good for plants that prefer dry and sunny conditions. They are also good for acid-loving plants (see below) that may be difficult to grow in most garden soils.

Acid-loving plants	
Camellia	*Pieris* 'Forest Flame'
Helleborus purpurascens	*Rhododendron*

feeding

Very few plants can sustain rapid growth without a boost of nutrients during the growing season, as the development of shoots, stems, leaves, and flowers can cause a huge drain on the plant's resources. This depletion is made even worse when flowering plants are deadheaded and the spent flower heads are taken away, as this deprives the plant of a valuable source of organic matter and nutrients. Unless some replacement nourishment is provided, the plant's performance and vigor will decline.

fertilizers

Artificial fertilizers vary greatly in the rate at which they release their nutrients. Described as slow- or quick-release, the essential difference between them lies in how soluble they are in water. The rate of release is also dependent on the size of the fertilizer particles: the smaller they are, the more rapidly they break down.

Dry fertilizer

The most common fertilizers come in the form of powder, granules, or pellets. They are used as a base dressing, added to the soil before sowing or planting, or to topdress established plants, such as shrubs or hungry feeders like chrysanthemums, during the growing season. The soil should be moist before applying a topdressing, and the plant will be able to take up the fertilizer most readily if it is incorporated into the topsoil.

| Release rates for some common fertilizers | |
Fertilizer type	Plant response
Slow-release (resin coat)	14–21 days
Quick-acting (topdressing)	7–10 days
Liquid feed (applied to soil)	5–7 days
Foliar feed (applied to foliage)	3–4 days

Liquid fertilizer

These come as a liquid concentrate or as granules or powder, which are diluted or dissolved in water. When preparing liquid fertilizer, it is essential to add the correct amount of water, following the manufacturer's recommendations. It is also important to mix it thoroughly and to keep the solution well agitated. These soluble fertilizers are applied with a watering can or hose, and are ideal for use on most plants.

Foliar fertilizer

These are specially formulated fertilizers used to correct specific nutrient deficiencies or meet particular needs. Sprays  containing magnesium will assist fruiting, and iron-based preparations are often used on acid-loving plants, such as azaleas and camellias, that are susceptible to iron deficiency when grown on slightly alkaline soils. Spray foliar feeds onto the leaves only on cloudy days to reduce the chances of leaf scorch.

when to feed

Plants growing in containers, such as hanging baskets and windowboxes, are particularly vulnerable because their roots are restricted and they have only a limited supply of food. Even if nutrients are present in the soil, they are effective only if the soil is moist enough. The best approach is to apply a regular liquid feed (every 10–14 days) once the plants have started to flower. For plants growing in garden soil, if they are repeat flowering, feed after the first flush of flowers; if they bloom only once each year, feed after flowering to promote good-quality flowers the following year.

The golden rules of feeding

- Always follow the manufacturer's directions.
- Only feed your plants when they are actively growing.
- Never feed plants that are dry unless you water the soil first.
- Do not apply fertilizer in bright sunlight, as this can lead to scorching.
- Wash off any concentrated fertilizer that is spilled directly onto the plant.

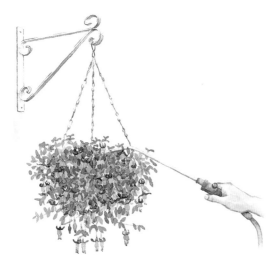

composting

Garden compost is another useful source of plant food. Well-rotted plant and animal waste not only provides nutrients (although not the high levels obtained from fertilizers), it also boosts the activity of earthworms and other beneficial creatures in the soil. Most garden and kitchen waste can be used, but aim for a balance of different materials.

1   Start by placing a layer of bulky material, such as wood shavings or finely shredded bark, about 4 inches deep, in the bottom of the compost bin. A container with a removable side is the easiest to work with.

2   Next add a layer of green material, such as grass mowings or cabbage leaves, about 8 inches deep. Alternating the layers like this will encourage rapid decomposition.

3   To accelerate the start of the composting process, sprinkle a compost accelerator over the layers; a cheaper alternative is to add a high-nitrogen fertilizer, such as sulfate of ammonia. Continue building up the pile, adding bulky and green material in alternate layers. After two weeks, turn the heap from top to bottom to allow it to compost evenly.

common nutrient deficiencies

	Symptoms	Causes	Susceptible plants	Control
Calcium	Overall reduction in growth, stunted shoot-tip growth, pale margin to the leaves, retarded root development.	Very low or very high soil pH, applying too much potassium, and high rainfall.	Most plants, but especially apples and tomatoes (fruit is damaged).	Apply calcium nitrate.
Iron	Pale yellow leaves, stunted shoot-tips and an overall reduction in growth.	High pH, and watering with tap water in "hard water" areas.	Acid-loving plants, including *Pieris*, *Camellia*, rhododendrons, and heathers.	Feed with fertilizer for acid-loving plants. Apply acid mulches, incorporate sulfur into the soil, or apply trace elements.
Magnesium	Yellow blotches between the veins on the lower (older) leaves.	Soils with low pH leaching from poor, freely draining soils, and loamless mediums with high levels of potassium.	Fruiting plants, especially tomatoes.	Apply Epsom salts as a liquid or foliar feed, 8 oz in 2½ gallons of water. To increase effectiveness, add a couple of drops of dishwashing liquid.
Manganese	Yellowing of the leaves.	Soil pH of 7.0 or more.	Apples, peaches, peas, and tomatoes.	Apply fertilizer containing manganese sulfate.
Nitrogen	Dull yellow leaves; thin spindly stems; overall reduction in growth.	Leaching from poor, freely draining soils, and loamless mediums.	Any plants.	Apply high-nitrogen fertilizer and compost.
Phosphate	Young foliage is dull bluish green, later turning yellow.	Low pH and high rainfall; heavy clay soils locking up the content of phosphates.	Potentially any plant, particularly seedlings.	Apply high-phosphorus fertilizer or superphosphate.
Potassium	Foliage turns bluish purple, later changing to yellow with brown, dead margins and tips to the leaves; reduced growth; and poor flowering and fruit.	Growing plants in light or peaty soils, or soils that have a high pH.	Apples, blackcurrants, and pears.	Apply potassium sulfate.

Malus 'Golden Hornet'

Pieris japonica 'Geisha'

Rhododendron narcissiforum

watering

Some plants consist of up to 90 percent water, which is constantly moving around them and being lost from pores in the leaves, in a process known as transpiration. Summer, for most plants, is a time of rapid growth. To sustain this, the plants need plenty of light and food and copious amounts of water; in particularly hot weather they may need watering twice each day to prevent wilting. Given the huge amount of work this may involve, it makes sense to conserve as much moisture as possible in the soil.

signs of water loss

In prolonged dry conditions, the amount of water lost through transpiration can exceed that taken in by the roots. Lost water must be replaced to keep the plant's cells filled and firm. If a plant has used up its water reserves it will begin to wilt. This manifests itself in the shedding of buds, premature drop of flowers or poor color and size in those that do open, early leaf loss, small fruits, and increased susceptibility to pests and diseases.

plants most at risk

Some types of plant are more susceptible than others to the effects of prolonged dry conditions. In general, the more sappy the plant and the softer its growth, the more vulnerable it is likely to be to drought. Bedding plants, for instance, will wilt rapidly in dry conditions. Young plants are also especially at risk, since their roots will not have penetrated far into the soil: these include newly planted vegetables, shrubs, or trees. Also, plants grown near mature trees, or in the dry soil next to a wall, need to be checked regularly for moisture loss.

preventing dry roots

How much water to apply is difficult to assess, because every soil is different. Always add enough to soak the soil to a reasonable depth, to encourage plant roots to follow the water downward. Plants subjected only briefly to drought should recover quickly if given a thorough soaking, ideally by allowing water to run gently onto the soil and soak in.

The effects of long-term drought are more difficult to rectify, and the focus should be on measures to prevent it from happening. Preparing the soil deeply with organic matter will help, as it provides a reservoir of moisture for roots. Mulching the surface, such as with bark (even black plastic), will reduce moisture loss through evaporation.

when to water

Choosing the correct time of day to water your plants can make huge savings in the amount of water lost through evaporation from the soil's surface. The soil is cool and the atmosphere is relatively moist in the early morning, and application then will allow the water maximum time to soak in and be of most use to the plants.

effective watering

1 Water needs to be delivered as close to the roots as possible. Drip-irrigation systems work well, with the low pressure and steady flow allowing the water to soak deep into the rooting zone.

2 Another simple but very efficient way of keeping water in the right area to benefit the plant is to create a shallow, saucer-shaped depression around the base of each plant. This way, any water that is applied into the depression is held in place until it can soak in.

plant requirements

Plants grown for their edible fruits have two critical watering periods. First, when they flower (to aid pollination and fruit set) and, second, after the fruit begins to show obvious signs of swelling. Other garden plants may have a higher-than-normal requirement for water because of their location—near walls or trees and shrubs, for instance, or because they have been planted in raised beds or other free-draining sites. Plants in pots, windowboxes, and hanging baskets must be watered at least daily, even when it rains.

water distribution

There are a number of specially designed appliances for watering your garden, with some being more suitable for large areas of lawn, and others for watering smaller beds and borders. For single plants, hand application is the easiest method.

Rain barrel
A useful means of collecting rainwater, essential for watering acid-loving plants in hard-water areas.

Watering can
The simplest and most basic method of watering, used for small areas or for young plants and seedlings that may be damaged by high-pressure jets, is a watering can.

controlling weeds

Once plants have become established and started to grow, they will usually cover the ground sufficiently or cast enough shade over the soil to suppress the germination and growth of weed seedlings. Until then, however, nature will need a helping hand, and any weeds that do appear must be removed on a regular basis.

weed problems

As weeds grow, they compete with crops and ornamental plants for light, nutrients, and water; they can also act as hosts to pests and diseases that may spread to the garden plants. Groundsel, for instance, may harbor the fungal diseases rust and mildew, as well as sap-sucking thrips and greenfly. Chickweed is a host of damaging red spider mite and whitefly. Some nightshade species host viruses and nematodes that can infect other members of the same family such as peppers, potatoes, and ornamental potato vines.

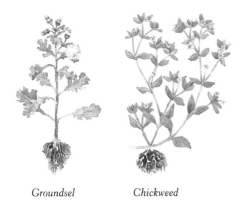

Groundsel　　　*Chickweed*

annual weeds

The old saying "one year's seeds make seven years' weeds" has now been the subject of scientific research and, unfortunately, is proving remarkably accurate. Some annual weeds can produce a population of 60,000 viable seeds per square yard each year, with the vast majority being found in the top 2 inches of soil.

Common annual weeds	
Annual bedstraw (*Galium aparine*)	Ivy-leaved speedwell (*Veronica hederifolia*)
Annual meadow grass (*Poa annua*)	Knotgrass (*Polygonum aviculare*)
Black nightshade (*Solanum nigrum*)	Pigweed (*Chenopodium album*)
Chickweed (*Stellaria media*)	Pineapple weed (*Matricaria matricarioides*)
Fumitory (*Fumaria officinalis*)	Shepherd's purse (*Capsella bursa-pastoris*)
Groundsel (*Senecio vulgaris*)	Small-flowered galansago (*Galansago parviflora*)
Hairy bittercress (*Cardamine hirsuta*)	

perennial weeds

These weeds live for many years, and digging them up is an effective way of dealing with them, as long as every bit of the root system is removed. If only a few weeds are present, dig them out with a trowel or tined implement. Do not throw perennial weeds on the compost heap, as they will simply regrow; always discard them.

Common perennial weeds	
Bindweed (*Convolvulus arvensis*)	Dandelion (*Taraxacum officinale*)
Broad-leaved dock (*Rumex obtusifolius*)	Elderberry (*Sambucus nigra*)
Clover (*Trifolium repens*)	Ground elder (*Aegopodium podagraria*)
Coltsfoot (*Tussilago farfara*)	Hawkweed (*Hieraceum*)
Creeping buttercup (*Ranunculus repens*)	Horsetail (*Equisetum arvense*)
Creeping thistle (*Cirsium arvense*)	Japanese knotweed (*Fallopia japonica*)
	Plantain (*Plantago major*)
	Quack grass (*Elymus repens*)

methods of weed control

There are four methods of weed control commonly available to the gardener: chemical, where a synthetic chemical is applied over the weeds to kill them; mulching, which involves covering the soil to deprive weeds of light; manual, where weeds are physically removed using some form of hand tool (see opposite); and mechanical, which is a method of chopping down or burying weeds using a rotary cultivator. Perennial weeds, which can persist for many years, are best dealt with chemically or by physically removing them.

chemicals

All chemicals used to kill weeds are known as herbicides. They are preferred by non-organic gardeners as their main method of weed control, and they are certainly one of the most effective ways of controlling persistent perennial weeds. The chemicals can be bought in concentrated form, to be diluted with water and then applied to plants through a watering can with a dribble bar attachment or a hose-end sprayer. Chemical fertilizers can also be bought as ready-to-use formulations. Herbicides available in sprays are normally intended for spraying onto individual, scattered weeds—as the weeds start to die, simply pull them out. In large areas, however, it is easier to dig over the soil to bury the weeds, but only if they are dead. Some herbicides are selective in that they will kill weeds in a lawn while leaving the grass unaffected, but you must make sure the spray does not come into contact with any cultivated plants.

mulching

As beneficial as organic mulches are on many levels in the garden, inorganic mulches are more effective for weed control because they form an impervious physical barrier. A typical inorganic mulch is heavy-duty black plastic. New plants can be introduced through slits cut into the plastic. Water the soil well before laying the plastic. However, inorganic mulches look rather unsightly, and in order to get the best of both worlds, this type of mulch is often covered with a thin layer of organic material to make it aesthetically pleasing.

In addition to helping to conserve moisture in the soil by minimizing evaporation and providing a decorative surface for garden beds, mulching is also a very effective technique for suppressing weed growth if properly applied. To work well against weeds, organic mulches, such as bark chips or used mushroom growing medium, must be at least 4 inches thick so enough sunlight is blocked out to prevent weed seeds in the soil germinating. Mulches tend to be less effective against established perennial weeds, unless the affected area can be completely covered until the weeds have died out. New planting must then be carried out with the mulch still in place to prevent regrowth. Any weed seeds that germinate in the surface of the mulch can be easily removed simply by pulling them out, as long as they are not left to develop root systems deep enough to reach the soil beneath.

thus starting the problem all over again. If you do not want to use some form of chemical control, then vigilance is the key: removing weeds as soon as you see them, when they are very young and have only shallow roots, will cause the least possible disturbance to the soil and any nearby established plants.

Combined control

The best way to control weeds is usually a combination of methods, especially where established perennial weeds are a problem. This involves spraying with an appropriate herbicide when the weeds are in full growth; as the weeds start to die, the area is dug over so the weeds are buried in the soil. When the next flush of weeds germinates in response to the ground being disturbed, and the young seedlings emerge, they can be sprayed with a chemical while they are at their most vulnerable and thus be quickly dispatched.

manual methods of weed control

Most weeds are found in the upper 2 inches of soil, and the simplest way to deal with them is to remove them physically. The principal disadvantage of this method of control is that it disturbs the soil, potentially exposing weed seeds to light and encouraging them to germinate,

hand tools for weed control

If you do not wish to use chemicals to control weeds in your garden, you will need to remove them by pulling or digging them out, or, if they are small enough, by hoeing them off at soil level. There are many tools available designed to cope with different types of weed. See below from top to bottom: a weeding knife is useful for removing weeds in cracks between paving and other narrow spaces; a daisy grubber removes large weeds from the lawn; a draw hoe works best for deep-rooted weeds; and a Dutch hoe is useful for chopping up shallow-rooted weeds.

spring protection

As the days lengthen in spring, many plants will still need protection from frost damage or damage from birds and other pests, to help advance growth and encourage earlier cropping or flowering. As they grow, many tall plants will also need supporting to stop the stems from bending over, and spring is the ideal time to set up a support structure, ready for the plant as it emerges from the soil.

protective structures

Cloches
Glass or rigid plastic covers offer the most effective form of frost protection. They can be purchased ready-made and placed over the plants that need protection (see below). However, bear in mind that they tend to lose temperature rapidly in the late afternoon and evening.

Fleece
Loosely woven or spun materials are now readily available. They don't provide a great deal of warmth but do maintain steady temperatures, making them ideal for short-term protection in early spring.

Plastic film
This material is inexpensive and easy to use. However, the air around the plants gets very hot during the day and loses heat rapidly during the night. Use for short-term protection and to give plants an early boost.

Screening
The very changeable weather conditions in the spring mean that young plants can be very easily damaged by sun scorch, particularly through glass. Some method of screening from very bright sunlight may well be necessary and should be applied earlier rather than later, after the damage has occurred. For small greenhouses, shade cloth or blinds made from split bamboo can be draped over the roof to filter the sun's rays, but they may interfere with the roof ventilators. If this is a problem, the glass can be painted or sprayed with shade paint, or with diluted white latex paint.

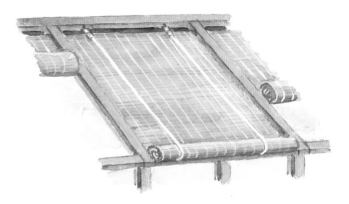

making a protective structure

A simple net, burlap, or plastic casing, held in place with stakes, will prevent wind and frost damage while still permitting air circulation and allowing the plants to breathe. When the weather improves, it can easily be removed.

1   Insert sturdy stakes (four is usually enough) into the soil around the plants to be protected, making sure the stakes are taller than the plants themselves.

2   Wrap net, burlap, or plastic sheets around the sides of the frame and secure with string, tied around the top, bottom, and middle of the casing.

supporting plants

As the weather starts to improve later in the season, the rapid growth of new plants can often take the gardener by surprise. To maintain the stature of your plants, it may be necessary to erect a support system to protect weak new stems from wind and rain damage. There are several different methods that can be used to support plants, depending on the size and habit of the plant, as well as its stage of growth.

Ties

Whatever method you use, you will need ties to attach the stem to the support structure. Garden string or twine is strong enough for most jobs and will stand up to a certain amount of wet weather. Plastic-coated wire is the strongest form of tie and has the added advantage of being waterproof.

Single stakes

Bamboo stakes are most commonly used and are ideal for single-stemmed annuals and perennials; however, they will rot over time, so you might prefer to invest in metal stakes, some of which have a loop at the top for slipping the stem through. Insert the stake into the ground and tie the stem of your plant to it in a figure-eight.

Ring supports

Clump-forming or multi-stemmed plants may need a larger structure, such as a ring or link stake. You can make your own by inserting rings of stakes and running string around them to hold the stems in place.

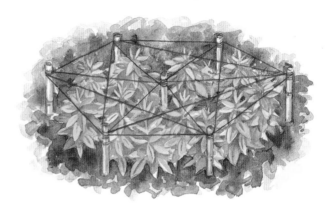

Aster amellus 'King George'

Helianthus mollis 'Monarch'

Plants that may need some support

African marigold
  (*Tagetes erecta*)

Aster

Bellflower (*Campanula*)

Black-eyed Susan vine
  (*Thunbergia alata*)

Coreopsis

Cornflower (*Centaurea*)

Dahlia

Delphinium

Hollyhock (*Alcea rosea*)

Larkspur (*Consolida ambigua*)

Painted tongue (*Salpiglossis*)

Peony (*Paeonia*)

Sunflower (*Helianthus*)

Paeonia officinalis 'China Rose'

making a
decorative path

One of the best materials for creating a path is concrete, which is both durable and easy to install. To make it more interesting, embed other materials into the surface so it is more pleasing to the eye, while still retaining its strength. One material that is often used this way is pebbles, and for a checkerboard effect, strips of wood can be embedded into the concrete at regular intervals.

MATERIALS & EQUIPMENT

pegs and brightly colored string

spade, rake, and garden roller

wooden retaining pegs 1 x 2 inches and retaining boards

galvanized nails, 3 inches long, and level

broken bricks or stone and sand

strips of wood 2 inches wide and 4 inches deep, enough for the sides and
the checkerboard effect; saw, hammer, and mallet

concrete (see step 8, page 237) and wheelbarrow

pebbles, about 3–4 inches in diameter

stiff-bristled brush and sheets of plastic

Creating the framework

1 Mark the route for your path with brightly colored string stretched between pegs. The pegs are set at least 3 inches wider than the intended edge of the path to allow for the retaining pegs inserted in step 3.

2 Dig out the soil within the colored string lines to form a shallow trench about 8 inches deep. Then rake the base of the trench level and compact it thoroughly using a garden roller.

3 Knock in retaining pegs along the string line marking the edge of the path, placing them about 3 feet apart all along the length—their purpose is to form an outside support to hold the retaining boards in place along the sides.

4 Lay out the retaining boards along both sides of the path and use 3-inch galvanized nails to attach them to the insides of the retaining pegs. Use a level to check that they are level both down the sides and across, from one side of the path to the other.

5 Now put a 6-inch layer of broken bricks or stone into the trench and compact it down to about 4 inches.

6 Add a base layer of sand over the bricks so it is about 2 inches deep and rake it over until it is level. Lightly compact it.

7 Next prepare the strips of wood that cross the path. Lay them in position over the sand and mark the angles where they need to be cut. Carefully cut them with a saw.

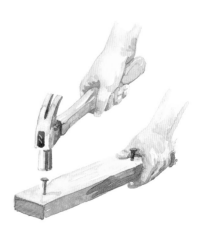

Wooden strips embedded in concrete can shrink and lift out; to prevent this from happening, knock 3-inch galvanized nails into the underside of each board, every 12 inches, leaving about 1½ inches protruding from the board. The heads of the nails will then set into the concrete as it dries which will prevent the boards from lifting out of the path.

Making the path

8   Make the concrete that will form the surface of the path. In a wheelbarrow, mix 1 part cement to 3½ parts sand and gravel (aggregate) and add water so it is thick and sticky. Add the concrete to the layer of sand, working in 3-foot sections, and rake and lightly compact it until it is roughly level.

9   For each section, while the concrete is still wet, push the wooden boards that will create the checkerboard effect into position by gently tapping them with a mallet until the upper surface is level with the concrete layer.

10   To finish off the decorative effect, push pebbles into the concrete, between the wooden strips, by gently wiggling them from side to side, up to about halfway, which should embed them securely into the concrete.

11   Repeat this whole process for each section, until the full length of the path is complete.

12   After about 4 hours, brush the pebbles and wooden boards with a stiff-bristled brush, which is regularly dipped in water—this will clean all traces of concrete from off the pebbles and boards, improving their appearance considerably.

13   Cover the path with plastic sheets for about 3 days to allow the concrete to cure.

14   After about a week, the pegs and retaining boards can be removed.

237

summer protection

It is not unreasonable to expect the best weather of the year during the summer months, but conditions may still pose a hazard to plants. In addition, pests are often attracted to the colorful and tasty flowers and fruits of this season, and deterrents will need to be put in place. Since summer is the main vacation season, measures may also need to be taken to make sure your plants survive short periods of neglect.

protecting blooms

The blooms of some plants are very delicate and are easily damaged by rain, dew, and mist, which may mark the petals. For many years, chrysanthemum and dahlia enthusiasts have "bagged" their prize blooms, which involves covering the young flower with a waxed paper bag as protection from moisture and dirt. Cover the flower as soon as the bud shows color—but not before, or the developing flower may become distorted.

holiday protection

If you do not want to return to an overgrown, neglected-looking garden after a vacation, make sure you carry out such tasks as mowing, cleaning up beds, fertilizing, and watering before you leave. Container, house, and bedding plants are the most vulnerable, since they have a limited root run and only small reserves of food and water.

Providing shade

For indoor plants, move the containers away from the windows so they are not in direct sunlight. Outdoor container plants can be pushed closer together so they provide shade for one another; grouped this way, they will also trap humidity to create their own microclimate. Larger container plants growing outdoors on a deck or patio can either be moved into a more shaded area, or if they are too heavy to move, a light screen of net or mesh can be draped over them to filter the sun's rays. Support the net on stakes to avoid damaging the plant.

Providing water

Small pot plants can be kept moist and humid by placing them on upturned saucers in a bathtub or sink with 1 inch of water in the bottom; the pots should not sit in the water or the roots will rot. For larger plants, place a bowl of water beside each one and run a wick of capillary matting or other absorbent material from the water into the soil. Another method of keeping plants moist is to water the plant well, then place the pot in a plastic bag. Tie the bag around the stem to prevent evaporation and recycle the water inside the bag. You can put the bag over the whole plant, but use this method only for short periods or the plant may start to rot.

protecting fruit

For many fruits the need for protection is not just from the elements; more frequently, marauding birds will enjoy the best of the season's crop if the ripening fruit is left unprotected. You can grow the fruit inside a permanent cage made with fine wire, or drape a soft string or nylon net over the plants and peg it in place to provide cover until picking has been completed.

Fruits that may need covering

Apricot	Currant	Nectarine
Blackberry	Gooseberry	Peach
Blueberry	Grape	Raspberry
Cherry	Loganberry	Strawberry

Cherry

Peach

supporting fruit trees

Fruit trees often need another form of protection, as in some years the burden of fruit may be so great that the stem and branches are unable to bear the weight and they may be physically damaged. The easiest way to prevent this is to select a sturdy stake that is at least 2 feet taller than the tree, and tie it in an upright position to the trunk or main stem. Use a commercial tree-tie or wrap the stem well with burlap to prevent rubbing or slipping. Run lengths of string from the top of the stake out to the branches, and tie them in place about two-thirds of the way along to provide support until the fruit is harvested.

protecting low-growing fruit

Low-growing plants often need protection from the soil, to keep them clean and prevent damage from soilborne pests and diseases. Strawberries produce their fruit very close to the ground; as the berries develop, they rest on the soil and are easily attacked by slugs and insects. Straw or plastic laid around the plants before the berries swell can overcome most of these problems.

repairs

Just as you take care of the plants in your garden, so must you regularly check and maintain all the equipment and the structures that play such an important part in the health and appearance of your garden. The beginning of spring is the ideal time to carry out repairs in preparation for the coming growing season.

greenhouse repairs

If any sheets of glass are broken, they should be replaced immediately. Without attention, in addition to the loss of heat, the wind will enter through the hole, causing more damage to the glass and the plants inside.

Aluminum alloy greenhouses

Remove the sprung metal clips that hold the glass in place, and take out the cracked or broken glass. Replace it with greenhouse or horticultural glass and return the metal slips.

Wooden greenhouses

With most wooden structures, the glass is held in place by a combination of a layer or "bed" of putty onto which the glass is pressed, and small glazing nails or "sprigs"; these hold the glass to the glazing bars.

1   Start by removing the old glazing sprigs with a pair of pliers, and carefully take out any broken sections of glass that remain. Then chop out any old dry putty with a hammer and glazing knife or chisel.

2   Spread an even layer of soft putty over the area where the old putty was removed from the glazing bars. Slide the new sheet of glass into place and carefully press it onto the bed of

putty. Care must be taken to apply pressure to the glass evenly or the sheet of glass will crack. Using a damp knife, remove any surplus putty from the glass and glazing bar.

3   Set the sheet of glass in position by knocking the new sprigs into the glazing bars. When the glass is secured, it can be cleaned with a damp cloth.

wood maintenance

Preserving wood

Wooden gates, fence posts, and other wooden garden structures will require regular applications of a suitable wood preservative to prolong the life of the wood and guard against extreme weather conditions, such as rain and sun scorch.

1   Remove any surface mold or lichen with a wire-bristled brush and make sure the wood is dry before painting begins—this is to make sure that the material will soak deeply into the wood for maximum protection.

2   Apply the preservative with an old paintbrush or garden sprayer, and take great care to protect any nearby plants by pulling them well away from the structure and covering them with sheets of plastic before any painting begins. It may be necessary to consider

applying a second coat for sections close to ground level or where the end grain of the wood is exposed.

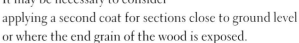

Repairing a rotten fence post

1 Pry out the nails holding the side panels into the post and ease the fence panels away from the post.

2 Dig around the base of the post until it is loose and lever it out of the ground. Then saw through as much of the post as necessary to remove all traces of rotten wood.

3 Refill the hole and compact the soil to make it as firm as possible, leaving the surface level. Then hammer the new fence spike into the soil.

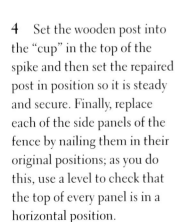

4 Set the wooden post into the "cup" in the top of the spike and then set the repaired post in position so it is steady and secure. Finally, replace each of the side panels of the fence by nailing them in their original positions; as you do this, use a level to check that the top of every panel is in a horizontal position.

garden tools

Early spring is a good time to thoroughly check over all gardening tools and equipment, as poorly maintained equipment tends to be ineffective and can damage plants by making ragged cuts, and may also be a danger to the gardener.

Cutting tools
Clean knives, loppers, and pruners with vinegar to remove any dried sap and dirt from the blades. Then wash them with water to remove all traces of vinegar and dry them. Finally, wipe the metal parts of the tools with an oily cloth to prevent rusting (see below).

The blades should be run through a sharpener; this will need to be done throughout the growing season if they are to maintain their effectiveness.

Cultivating tools
These can be cleaned with an oily rag (see below), and any splits or splinters in wooden handles should be smoothed by rubbing them with sandpaper.

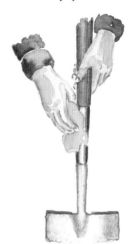

243

making a sink garden

Tubs, sinks, and troughs of various kinds can be recycled to make excellent containers for plants, and by adding a special coating, they can be made to look like natural stone. Alpines provide an excellent display for many years in containers such as an old earthenware sink, and are one of the most diverse groups of plants grown. Low-growing or mat-forming shrubs and conifers are also good subjects, with some covering the surface and others trailing over the rim. Place the sink in position before you start work since it may be too heavy to move once planting is complete.

MATERIALS & EQUIPMENT

old sink

wire brush and mild detergent

sponge, sand, and water

cement, sand, and peat

stiff-bristled paintbrush

pot shards

capillary matting

free-draining loam-based potting medium

spade

trowel

suitable plants (see page 247)

gravel mulch

1   Thoroughly clean the sink using a mild detergent and a wire brush, scrubbing the outside and rim of the sink, as well as the inside.

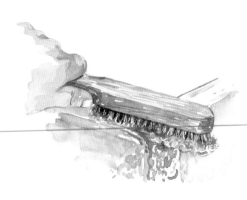

2   Clean the sink again, including the top and the upper inside edge, using a sponge dipped into a paste made of equal parts fine sand and water. This will scour the surface of the sink and help the coating to bind to it.

3   To create a weathered-stone look, make a coating using equal parts of cement, sand, and peat moss. Thoroughly mix the ingredients together, then gradually add enough water to form a stiff paste.

4   Using an old stiff-bristled paintbrush, spread a ¼-inch layer of the coating over the surface of the sink, including the rim and the top 3 inches of the inside. Leave the coating to dry.

5   After two or three days, apply a second layer ½ inch thick and leave this to dry.

6   Place a layer of pot shards, 3 inches deep, in the bottom of the sink, and cover them with a sheet of capillary matting. This will prevent the soil from being washed down into the shards and impeding drainage.

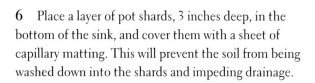

7 Fill the sink with free-draining soil. Firm the surface gently with the spade. Top up with more soil as necessary to fill the sink to within 2 inches of the rim.

8 Using a trowel, dig planting holes and place the new plants in them, leaving the top of each root ball slightly high. Firm them in gently.

9 Position the trailing species near the edges of the sink, so they can spill over the sides as they grow. During planting, check that each plant has enough room to develop comfortably. Avoid overcrowding or the plants will have to struggle to survive.

10 When planting is finished, spread a 1-inch layer of fine gravel over the surface of the soil between the plants. To protect the plants while you do this, cover them temporarily with inverted pots. The gravel mulch will help to retain moisture in the soil, improve surface drainage in winter, inhibit the germination of weed seeds, and prevent slugs from attacking the plants.

Alpines suitable for growing in sinks and troughs

Arenaria nevadensis	*Helichrysum coralloides*	*Raoulia australis*
Carduncellus rhaponticoides	*Juniperus communis* 'Compressa'	*Salix reticulata*
Cyclamen coum	*Lewisia* hybrids	*Saxifraga* 'Tumbling Waters'
Daphne petraea 'Grandiflora'	*Petrophytum caespitosum*	*Sedum spathulifolium* 'Cape Blanco'
Erinus alpinus	*Potentilla tommasiniana*	
Gentiana septemfida	*Ramonda myconi*	

soil management

Soil, although we often take it for granted, is the most important resource in the garden and is a very complex material. It can be very delicate and must always be well managed and cared for if it is to provide an adequate environment for plant growth. A basic understanding of your soil type is the first step toward creating the best possible conditions for all the plants in your garden. Good soil management includes the use of fertilizer and manure to improve quality and texture, planned crop rotation to prevent the invasion of pests and diseases and help return nutrients to the soil, and the addition of organic matter to improve moisture retention. All these measures will help to improve the soil's ability to support plant life.

improving your soil

To get the most from your soil, you must first have a thorough understanding of its structure. The gardener need only be concerned with the first two levels of soil. The top level, referred to as "topsoil," is the biologically active area, occupied by millions of bacteria, fungi, insects, worms, and other life forms. It is usually dark in color and can vary in depth from 2 inches in more chalky soils, to 3 feet or more. The layer lying below this is called "subsoil" and can be distinguished by its paler color, caused by a lack of organic matter; it can also be identified by orange and yellow flecks of iron oxide.

determining your soil type

It is important to identify the nature of the soil in your garden, since this factor can have a significant effect on the growth of your plants. Once you have categorized your soil, there are various methods you can employ to improve the situation (unless it is perfect) and create a more healthy environment for your plants to grow in.

Texture
The first thing to do is to test the texture of your soil, because any variations can significantly affect its drainage capabilities. Simply pick up a handful from the garden and rub it between your fingers and thumb to determine its characteristics.

Clay: This is a heavy, sticky soil that can be rolled into shape. Clay suffers from poor drainage but is rich in plant food. To improve its quality, you need to open it up by digging in manure, compost, gravel, or lime.

Sandy: Characterized by a light, dry texture, this soil is free-draining, but tends to lack essential nutrients and needs frequent watering. Improve this soil by removing large stones and adding manure and fertilizer.

Soil pH
Measured on a scale from 0 to 14, anything above 7 is alkaline and below 7 is acidic; 7 indicates neutral soil. Use a special kit to test your soil pH, matching the prepared sample with the color scale provided; dark green indicates alkalinity, gradually changing to orange for acidic soils. A reading of 6.5 is ideal, as most plants prefer a slightly acidic soil. If your soil is too acidic, it probably lacks phosphorus, and an application of lime will raise alkalinity. To raise the acidic content, add ground sulphur to your soil.

fertilizer and manure

Applying fertilizer and manure is all part of the process of soil preparation and must be done before any planting. Most garden soil will need a certain amount of improvement in order to sustain the plants. The main nutrients needed to improve plant growth are nitrogen, phosphorus, and potassium, and these are available as both fertilizers and manures. You can either apply these nutrients separately or use a general fertilizer that contains all three. In most regions where plants are established, nitrogen fertilizer, for instance, may be better applied in early spring than in late fall. Resulting new soft growth of plants can be injured later by freezing.

Bulky organic manure

Incorporating quantities of bulky organic matter provides nutrients and fiber for garden soil, as well as improving the water content. Green vegetation and manures with animal content will provide some nutrients almost immediately, but very little fiber. The more woody and fibrous materials are better for opening heavy soils, and on lighter soils they improve moisture retention. Long-term improvements occur as they decompose, contributing to the formation of humus, which then absorbs other applied nutrients.

Percentage of nutrients (approximately)

Material	Nitrogen N	Phosphate P	Potash K
Bark	0.3	0.2	0.2
Garden compost	1.5	2.0	0.7
Leaf mold	0.4	0.2	0.3
Manure—chicken	2.0	2.0	1.0
Manure—cow	0.6	0.3	0.7
Manure—horse	0.7	0.5	0.6
Manure—pig	0.6	0.6	0.4
Manure—sheep	0.6	0.3	0.7
Manure—turkey	2.0	1.5	1.0
Mushroom medium	0.6	0.5	0.9
Peat moss	0.7	0.2	0.2
Sawdust	0.3	0.2	0.2
Seaweed	0.6	0.3	1.0
Sewage sludge	1.0	0.6	0.2
Spent hops	1.1	0.3	0.1
Straw	0.5	0.2	0.7

Fertilizers

These can be applied as base dressings, when an application of fertilizer or bulky organic matter is added to the soil surface and incorporated before planting or seed sowing begins. They can also be introduced into the soil as a topdressing: fertilizer or bulky organic matter is applied to the soil surface and incorporated around the base of the plant once it is in position. Fast-action fertilizers are good for giving your plant a quick boost and are easier to control; however, the application of slow-release types is far less time-consuming.

	% Nutrient	Type	Action
Nitrogen N			
Ammonium nitrate	34	inorganic	fast
Ammonium sulfate	21	inorganic	fast
Bonemeal	5	organic	slow
Cottonseed meal	7	organic	fairly fast
Dried blood	12	organic	fairly fast
Hoof and horn	12	organic	fairly fast
Nitrate of potash	44	inorganic	fast
Nitrate of soda	16	inorganic	fast
Phosphate P			
Basic slag	14	inorganic	slow
Bonemeal, steamed	30	organic	slow
Superphosphate	19	inorganic	fast
Potash K			
Muriate of potash	53	inorganic	fast
Nitrate of potash	44	inorganic	fast
Sulfate of potash	50	inorganic	fast

Green manure

Instead of using compost and manure, you can grow plants to incorporate into the soil as an improver. Plant them in the fall and dig into the soil once they have grown to 8 inches. Green manure returns more to the ground than it has taken out and will eventually form humus within the soil. Choose plants with a rapid growth rate that mature quickly, such as legumes.

Green manure	% Nitrogen
Borage	1.8
Comfrey	1.7
Mustard	2.0
Red clover	3.0
Ryegrass	1.2

soil cultivation

The ideal time to dig is in the fall or early winter, when the soil is often quite dry and not as wet as when the rain and snow start. Lighter soil, such as sandy loam, should not be cultivated over the winter, as the wind, rain, and frost can damage the soil structure. Digging opens up the soil to allow air penetration and helps to bury annual weeds and plant debris, which returns nutrients back into the soil, improving drainage and the formation of a deeper root system.

simple digging

Simple digging is where a spadeful of soil is lifted and turned over as it is dropped back into its original position. This technique is useful for clearing the surface of the soil and for digging around existing plants, as it does not disturb their roots.

single digging

1   Dig a trench about 10 to 12 inches wide and the depth of the spade or fork, and move the soil.

2   Facing the trench, dig a second trench and use the soil from this one to fill in the one made in the previous step.

3   Twist the spade a little when putting the soil into the first trench so that the upper layers of soil and any weeds go to the bottom.

4   Repeat this process down the length of your plot, filling in the final trench with the soil taken out of the first trench.

double digging

Use a digging spade and a fork. Turn so that you are digging across the trench and roughly divide the trench into three times the width of the spade's blade; it is helpful to mark the area with garden twine and pegs. Make sure each trench is about the same size, so that a similar amount of soil is moved from trench to trench and the plot remains level. Try to avoid mixing the topsoil with the subsoil, as it is better to concentrate your efforts on increasing the fertility of the topsoil, though some gardeners believe that mixing the two layers will eventually help to increase the depth of fertile soil.

1 Start by digging out a trench about 2 feet wide and the depth of the spade's blade. As you remove the soil, place it in a pile to one side of the trench.

2 Stand in the trench and use a fork to break up the bottom to the full depth of its tines. The soil has now been cultivated to an overall depth of about 20 inches.

3 Mark another 2-foot-wide trench, parallel to the first one. Soil taken from the second trench can now be used to fill in the first one.

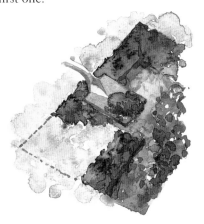

4 Fork over the second trench and fill in as before. Continue this technique up to the last trench, filling this one in with the soil from the first trench.

zero cultivation system

A growing system that is increasing in popularity is a system of zero cultivation. The aim is to incorporate large quantities of organic matter into the soil by double digging; then the soil is left relatively undisturbed. The reasoning behind this system is that cultivating the soil creates an ideal environment for the germination of weed seeds, as well as destroying the soil's natural structure and causing a loss of plant nutrients. This system minimizes problems with weed control, because if you don't dig the soil, the seeds cannot be brought up from its lower depths. The usual method of weed control is to use a surface covering of organic mulch to suppress weed-seed germination by causing a lack of daylight. The mulch is incorporated into the soil by the activity of earthworms, which in turn increases humus content and fertility, as well as improving the soil structure naturally. These mulches also create more even soil temperatures, which encourages plant growth by reducing the stress on the plant.

making a compost bin

A compost bin, made to look like a traditional beehive, is both practical and decorative. Making a feature of your bin is particularly useful in a small garden where it would be difficult to hide an unsightly one. This construction is relatively easy to make and can be painted to fit in with your garden scheme. Almost any form of vegetable material is suitable for making compost, provided it is not diseased or contaminated with chemicals. Grass clippings, soft pruning and hedge clippings, leaves, annual weeds, and straw, vegetable, and household waste are all suitable.

MATERIALS & EQUIPMENT

sawed lumber (see steps, over page)

exterior-grade plywood (see steps, over page)

galvanized nails, 2 inches long

waterproof glue

2 roof bolts, 3 inches long

2 wooden pegs, 6 inches long

1 quart rubberized paint

1 quart microporous paint

glossary

A

Aerate

To loosen soil, either by physical or mechanical means, to allow the penetration of air.

Algae

Primitive green plants that form a scumlike layer in ponds.

Alpine

A plant originating in mountainous regions; the term is often applied to rock garden plants.

Alternate

Buds or leaves that occur at different levels on opposite sides of the stem.

Annual

A plant that completes its reproduction cycle in one year.

Aquatic

Any plant that grows in water (may be anchored or free floating).

Axil

The angle between a leaf and stem.

Axillary bud

A bud that occurs in a leaf axil.

B

Bare-root

Plants with no soil around their roots. Bare-rooted plants are usually grown in a field before being dug up for sale.

Basal

A shoot or bud arising from the base of a stem or plant.

Base dressing

An application of fertilizer or organic matter incorporated into the soil around the base of a plant.

Bedding plants

Plants arranged in mass displays (beds) to form a colorful but temporary display.

Bed system

A highly productive system of growing vegetables in closely spaced rows to form blocks of plants.

Biennial

A plant that completes its life cycle in two growing seasons. It produces roots and leaves in the first year followed by flowers and fruit in the next.

Bleeding

The excessive flow of sap, usually from plants pruned in spring. Bleeding can often be minimized by pruning when plants are in full leaf.

Bog plant

A plant that prefers to grow in damp soil conditions.

Bolt

The premature flowering and seed production of a cropping plant.

Branch

A shoot growing directly from the main stem of a woody plant.

Brassica

Belonging to the cabbage family.

Broadcasting

The technique of spreading fertilizer or seeds randomly.

Broad-leaved

Deciduous or evergreen plants that have flat, broad leaves.

Bud

A condensed shoot containing an embryonic shoot or flower.

Bud union

The point where a cultivar is budded onto a rootstock. Most often employed to control the ultimate height of a plant.

Bulb

A storage organ consisting of thick, fleshy leaves arranged on a compressed stem.

C

Callus

The plant tissue that forms as a protective cover over a cut or wounded surface.

Chamfer

A 45° bevel, made along the edge of a piece of wood.

Chilling

A period of low temperature, about 36°F, required by some plants during dormancy to stimulate flower development later in the growing season.

Cloche

A clear structure used for warming the soil or for protecting plants.

Cold frame

A low, clear, portable or permanent structure used for protecting plants and acclimatizing them to normal garden conditions.

Collar

The point on a plant where the roots begin at the base of the main stem, or the swollen area where a branch joins the main stem.

Compost

Well-rotted organic matter, such as garden or kitchen waste, used to improve the structure and quality of garden soil.

Conifer

A classification of plants that have naked ovules, often borne in cones, and narrow, needlelike foliage.

Coppicing

The severe pruning of plants to ground level on an annual basis.

Cordon

A plant, often a tree, that is trained to produce fruiting spurs from a main stem.

Crop rotation

A system of moving crops in a planned cycle to improve growth and help control pests and diseases.

Crown

The growing point of an herbaceous perennial originating at soil level.

Cultivar

A plant form that originated in cultivation rather than from the wild.

Cutting

A portion of a plant used for propagation.

D

Deadheading

The deliberate removal of dead flower heads. Deadheading often prolongs a plant's flowering period.

Deciduous

Plants that produce new leaves in the spring and shed them in the fall.

Disbudding

Removal of unwanted buds to produce fewer, but much larger, flowers.

Division

A technique used to increase the number of plants by splitting up a single parent plant into smaller units for replanting.

Dormancy

A period of reduced growth, usually extending from late fall through the winter months and finishing as the weather warms in spring.

Drill

A narrow straight line made in the soil for sowing seeds into (a seed trench).

E

Earthing up

A process of mounding up the soil around the base of a plant.

Espalier

A tree trained to produce several horizontal tiers of branches all growing from a vertical main stem.

Evergreen

Plants that retain their actively growing leaves through the winter.

F

Fan

A tree or shrub trained to create a network of branches spreading out from the main stem.

Feathered

A young tree with small lateral branches.

Fertile

A soil rich in nutrients and biological life.

Fertilizer

An organic or inorganic compound used to help plants to grow.

Fibrous roots

The fine, multibranched roots of a plant.

Floating mulch

A sheet of plastic or woven material used for protecting plants from frost.

Force

Induce plants to grow earlier than usual.

Formative pruning

The pruning of young plants designed to establish a desired plant shape and branch structure.

Framework

The main permanent branch structure of a woody plant.

Fruit

The seed-bearing vessel on a plant.

Fungicide

A chemical used to control fungal disease in plants.

G

Germination

The development of a seed into a plant.

Grafting

A propagation method that involves the joining of two or more separate plants together.

Graft union

The point where a cultivar is grafted onto a rootstock.

Ground cover

The term used to describe low-growing plants.

H

Half hardy

A plant that can tolerate low temperatures but is killed by hard frost.

Hardy

A plant that can tolerate temperatures below freezing without protection.

Herbaceous

A non-woody plant with an annual top and a perennial root system or storage organ.

Herbicide

A chemical used to kill weeds.

Humus

The organic residue of decayed organic material.

I

Inorganic

A man-made chemical compound (one that does not contain carbon).

Insecticide

A chemical used to kill insects.

Irrigation

A general term used for the application of water to soil and plants.

L

Lateral

A side shoot arising from an axillary bud.

Layering

A propagation technique where roots are formed on a stem before it is detached from the parent plant.

Leaching

The loss of nutrients by washing them through the soil.

Leader

The main dominant shoot or stem of the plant (usually the terminal shoot).

Legume

A member of the pea family that bears seeds in pods.

Lime

An alkaline substance formed from calcium.

Loam

A soil with equal proportions of clay, sand, and silt.

M

Maiden

A young (one-year-old) budded or grafted tree or bush.

Marginal plant

A plant that prefers to grow in damp soil conditions or partially submerged in water.

Mulch

A layer of material applied to cover the soil.

Mutation

A plant change or variation occurring by chance, often referred to as a "sport."

N

Nematode

A microscopically small wormlike organism that can be introduced into the garden to attack specific pests and reduce the need to use chemical pesticides.

Nutrients

The minerals (naturally occurring or introduced in the form of fertilizers) used to feed plants.

O

Opposite

Plants in which leaves, buds, or stems are arranged in pairs directly opposite one another.

Organic

Materials derived from decomposed animal or plant remains.

Ovule

The body in a seed-bearing plant that contains the egg cell. It is the egg cell that will develop into the seed once fertilization takes place.

Oxygenator

An aquatic plant that releases oxygen into the water. Lack of oxygen in garden pond water can lead to the poor growth of aquatic plants and poor health in fish.

P

Peat

Decayed mosses, rushes, or sedges.

Perennial

A plant that has a life cycle of three years or more.

Pesticide

A chemical used to control pests.

pH

The level of acidity or alkalinity in a soil, measured on a scale of 1 to 14; 7 is neutral, below 7 is acid, and above 7 is alkaline.

Pinching out

The removal (with finger and thumb) of the growing point of a plant to encourage the development of lateral shoots.

Pollarding

The severe pruning of the main branches of a tree or shrub to the main stem or trunk.

Propagation

Different techniques used to multiply a number of plants.

Propagator
A structure in which plants are propagated.

Pruning
Cutting plants to improve their growth, to train them to grow in a particular way or to restrict their growth to prevent them becoming too large for their allocated space.

R

Renewal pruning
A method of pruning based on the systematic replacement of lateral fruiting branches.

Rhizome
A specialized underground stem that lies horizontally in the soil.

Root ball
The combined root system and the surrounding soil or growing medium of a plant. Plants are often sold in this form, wrapped in burlap.

Root pruning
The cutting of the roots of live plants to control their vigor or ultimate height.

Rootstock
The root system onto which a cultivar is budded or grafted.

Runner
A stem that grows horizontally close to the ground, such as in strawberry plants.

S

Sap
The solution of mineral salts, sugars, and other nutrients that circulates in and nourishes a plant.

Scale
A modified leaf of a bulb, used in propagation.

Scion
The propagation material taken from a cultivar or variety that is to be used for budding or grafting.

Shoot
A stem or branch of a plant.

Shrub
A woody stemmed plant.

Side shoot
A shoot arising from a stem or branch.

Sport
See Mutation.

Spur
A short flower- or fruit-bearing branch.

Standard
A tree or bush with a clear stem of at least 6 feet.

Stooling
The severe pruning of plants to within 4–6 inches of ground level on an annual basis.

Stratification
The storage of seed in cold or warm conditions to overcome dormancy.

Sucker
A shoot arising from below ground level.

T

Taproot
The main large, anchoring root of a plant.

Tender
A plant that is killed or damaged by low temperatures, usually 14°F.

Tendril
A thin, twisting, stemlike structure used by some climbing plants to support themselves.

Thatch
A layer of dead organic matter on the soil surface of a lawn.

Tilth
A fine crumbly layer of surface soil.

Tip pruning
Cutting back the growing point of a shoot to encourage the development of lateral shoots.

Topdressing
An application of fertilizer or bulky organic matter added to the soil surface.

Transplanting
Moving plants from one site to another to give them more growing room or to move them to a more suitable site.

U

Union (graft union)
Where a cultivar is grafted onto a rootstock.

V

Vegetative growth
Non-flowering stem growth.

W

Whip
A young (one-year-old) tree with no lateral branches.

Whorl
The arrangement of three or more leaves, buds, or shoots arising from the same level of a plant.

Wilt
The partial collapse of a plant due to water loss or root damage.

useful addresses

Nurseries and Plant Specialists

Alberta Nurseries & Seeds
P.O. Box 446
Bowden
Alberta, T0M 0M0
Canada
403-224-3544
www.gardenersweb.ca

W. Atlee Burpee & Co.
300 Park Avenue
Warminster, PA 18974
800-333-5808
www.burpee.com

Avant Gardens
710 High Hill Road
Dartmouth, MA 02747
508-998-8819
www.avantgardensNE.com

Bluestone Perennials
7211 Middle Ridge Road
Madison, OH 44057
800-852-5243
www.bluestoneperennials.com

Canyon Creek Nursery
3527 Dry Creek Road
Oroville, CA 95965
530-533-2166
www.canyoncreeknursery.com

Carroll Gardens
444 East Main Street
Westminster, MD 21157
800-638-6334
www.carrollgardens.com

Catnip Acres Herb Farm
67 Christian Street
Oxford, CT 06478
203-888-5649

The Cook's Garden
P.O. Box C5030
Warminster, PA 18974
800-457-9703
www.cooksgarden.com

Dabney Herbs
P.O. Box 22061
Louisville, KY 40252
502-893-5198
www.dabneyherbs.com

Dutch Gardens
144 Intervale Road
Burlington, VT 05401
888-821-0448
www.dutchgardens.com

Gurney's Seed & Nursery Co.
Customer Service
P.O. Box 4178
Greendale, IN 47025
513-354-1492
www.gurneys.com

Jackson & Perkins
1 Rose Lane
Medford, OR 97501
1-877-322-2300
www.jacksonandperkins.com

Johnny's Selected Seeds
955 Benton Avenue
Winslow, ME 04901
877-564-6697
www.johnnyseeds.com

Lilypons Water Gardens
6800 Lily Pons Road
Adamstown, MD 21710
800-999-5459
www.lilypons.com

Logee's Greenhouses
141 North Street
Danielson, CT 06239
888-330-8038
www.logees.com

Matterhorn Nursery
227 Summit Park Road
Spring Valley, NY 10977
845-354-5986
www.matterhornnursery.com

Miller Nurseries
5060 West Lake Road
Canandaigua, NY 14424
800-836-9630
www.millernurseries.com

Mountain Valley Growers
38325 Pepperweed Road
Squaw Valley, CA 93675
559-338-2775
www.mountainvalley
  growers.com

Musser Forests Inc.
1880 Route 119 North
Indiana, PA 15701
800-643-8319
www.musserforests.com

Park Seed Company
1 Parkton Avenue
Greenwood, SC 29647
800-213-0076
www.parkseed.com

Plant Delights Nursery
9241 Sauls Road
Raleigh, NC 27603
919-772-4794
www.plantdelights.com

The Rosemary House
1120 South Market Street
Mechanicsburg, PA 17055
717-697-5111
www.therosemaryhouse.com

Sandy Mush Herb Nursery
316 Surrett Cove Road
Leicester, NC 28748
828-683-2014
www.sandymushherbs.com

Stokes Seeds Inc.
P.O. Box 548
Buffalo, NY 14240
800-396-9238
www.stokeseeds.com

Thompson & Morgan
220 Faraday Avenue
Jackson, NJ 08527
800-274-7333
www.thompson-morgan.com

Van Engelen Inc.
23 Tulip Drive
Bantam, CT 06750
860-567-8734
www.vanengelen.com

André Viette Farm & Nursery
994 Long Meadow Road
Fisherville, VA 22939
800-575-5538
www.viette.com

Waterford Gardens
74 East Allendale Road
Saddle River, NJ 07458
201-327-0721
www.waterfordgardens.com

Wavecrest Nursery and Landscaping
2509 Lakeshore Drive
Fennville, MI 49408
888-869-4159
www.wavecrestnursery.com

Wayside Gardens
1 Garden Lane
Hodges, SC 29695
800-213-0379
www.waysidegardens.com

We-Du Natives
2055 Polly Spout Road
Marion, NC 28752
828-738-8300
www.we-du.com

White Flower Farm
P.O. Box 50
Litchfield, CT 06759
800-503-9624
www.whiteflowerfarm.com

Woodlanders
1128 Colleton Avenue
Aiken, SC 29801
803-648-7522
www.woodlanders.net

Yucca Do Nursery
P.O. Box 907
Hempstead, TX 77445
979-826-4580
www.yuccado.com

Planters and Garden Structures

Brooklyn Botanic Garden
1000 Washington Avenue
Brooklyn, NY 11225
718-623-7200
www.bbg.org

Crate & Barrel
Find a store near you at
www.crateandbarrel.com

Florentine Craftsmen
46–24 28th Street
Long Island City, NY 11101
718-937-7632
www.florentinecraftsmen.com

Gardener's Supply Co.
128 Intervale Road
Burlington, VT 05401
888-833-1412
www.gardeners.com

Kinsman Company
P.O. Box 428
Pipersville, PA 18947
800-733-4129
www.kinsmangarden.com

Master Garden Products
3223 C Street NE #1
Auburn, WA 98002
800-574-7248
www.mastergarden
    products.com

Smith & Hawken
P.O. Box 8690
Pueblo, CO 81008
800-940-1170
www.smithandhawken.com

Treillage
418 East 75th Street
New York, NY 10021
212-535-2288
www.treillageonline.com

Trellis Structures
60 River Street
Beverly, MA 01915
888-285-4624
www.trellisstructures.com

Paint, Lumber, and Building Supplies

Ace Hardware Corporation
Find a store near you at
www.acehardware.com

Benjamin Moore & Co
51 Chestnut Ridge Road
Montvale, NJ 07645
www.benjaminmoore.com

The Home Depot
Find a store near you at
www.homedepot.com

Lowe's
Find a store near you at
www.lowes.com

credits

l. = left, c. = center, a. = above, b. = below, r. = right

The photographer, Anne Hyde, wishes to make the following acknowledgments: English Hurdle, Stoke St. Gregory, Somerset, for the loan of wattle fencing; Mr and Mrs Coote, 40 Osler Road, Headington, Oxford; Judy Brown, Masham Manor, East Molesey; Meg Blumson, 20 St Peter's Road, Cirencester; Jean and Ian Housley; The *Gardening Which* Garden, Capel Manor, Enfield; Fran Donovan; Robin Allen; Michael Goulding, Hipkins, Herts; Ruth Thornton, Balfour Road, Northampton; Jon Tye, Lea Gardens, Derby; Malley Terry, Hillgrove Crescent, Kidderminster; Mr and Mrs Nicholas Calvert, Walton Poor, Surrey; Benington Lordship, Herts; Sandy Lodge, Beds; Mrs Rogers, Riverhill House, Kent; The Beale Arboretum, Herts; Milton Lodge, Somerset; Westonbirt Arboretum, Gloucs; H. Groffman, St Quintin Avenue, London; Peter Aldington, Garden Designer of Turn End, Haddenham, Bucks; Vivien and John Savage, Stockgrove Park, Bucks; Mr and Mrs D. Ingall, Irthlingborough, Northants; Mr and Mrs Douglas Fuller, The Crossing House, Shepreth, Cambridge; Merle and Peter Williams, Ickleford, Herts; Glen and Beverley Williams, Ickleford, Herts; Mrs Easter, Harpenden, Herts; Mr and Mrs Siggers, Wichert, Ford, Bucks; Lucy Sommers, 13 Queen Elizabeth Walk, London; Ivan Meers and David Boyer; Heather Montgomery, Wisteria Cottage, Maidwell, Northants; Mr and Mrs Try, Favershams Meadow, Bucks; Vanessa and Vinda Saax; Mrs Huntingdon, The Old Rectory, Sudborough, Northants; Charles Paddick; Capel Manor, Enfield, Herts; Clifton Nurseries, Clifton Villas, Little Venice, London.

All photographs taken by Anne Hyde except for the following: **Endpapers** Melanie Eclaire/Sticky Wicket wildlife garden near Dorchester, designed and created by Peter and Pam Lewis (www.sticky wicketgarden.co.uk); **7** Melanie Eclare/Jim Reynolds' garden "Butterstream," Co. Meath, Ireland; **10** Melanie Eclare/Daphne Shackleton's garden in Co. Cavan, Ireland; **14 al & bcl** Jerry Harpur; **14 bl** Jerry Harpur/Beth Chatto; **14 br** Melanie Eclare; **24 & 25** Jerry Harpur; **38, 53, & 54** Marianne Majerus; **57 a** Jerry Harpur; **58 & 59** © Andrew Lawson; **62 b** Jerry Harpur; **65** © Andrew Lawson/Chilcombe House, Dorset; **82** Pia Tryde; **83** © Andrew Lawson; **95 bl, bc, & br** Jerry Harpur; **109 l** Pia Tryde; **109 r** Jerry Harpur; **116 br** Melanie Eclare; **125 a & c** Jerry Harpur; **128** Jonathan Buckley; **129** Marcus Harpur; **135 l & cl** Jerry Harpur; **135 cr, 137 r, & 141 r** Marcus Harpur; **144 l & ar** Stephen Robson; **144 br** © Andrew Lawson; **168 & 169** Andrea Jones; **180 all & 206–207 all** Jerry Harpur; **216 al** Marianne Majerus; **216 bl** Caroline Arber; **216 r** © Andrew Lawson; **224 all, 233 all, & 239 l** Jerry Harpur.

All projects designed by Steven Bradley except the Compost Bin Project—designed by George Carter and photographed at the *Gardening Which* garden at Capel Manor.

Also thanks to the Principal at Capel Manor Horticulture Centre, Bullsmoor Lane, Enfield, and the Editor of *Gardening Which*, P.O. Box 44, Hertford X, SG14 1SH.

index

Page numbers in *italics* refer to illustrations.

acknowledgments

In putting this book together, I would like to thank a whole host of people.

In particular, I am most grateful to Toria Leitch and Caroline Davison for working

my fingers to the bone, and my wife Val Bradley for keeping a straight face while

checking my grammar. I would also like to thank Anne Hyde for her excellent

photographs and Ashley Western and Prue Bucknall for their design input.

CONVERSION TABLE

Inch	Cm	Feet	M
½	1	2	0.6
¾	2	3	0.9
1	2.5	3 ft 3 in	1
1½	3.5	4	1.2
2	5	5	1.5
2½	6	6	1.8
3	8	7	2.2
3½	9	8	2.5
4	10	9	2.7
5	13	10	3
6	15	15	4.5
7	17	20	6
8	20	30	9
10	25	40	12
12	30	50	15
18	45		
20	50		